Mappa Mundi

Shelagh Stephenson

Shelagh Stephenson was born in Northumberland and read drama at Manchester University. Her first stage play, *The Memory of Water*, premiered at Hampstead Theatre in 1996 and subsequently transferred to the West End, where it won an Olivier Award for Best Comedy in 2000. Her second play, *An Experiment With An Air Pump*, opened at the Royal Exchange Theatre in Manchester. It was joint recipient of the Peggy Ramsay Award and later transferred to the Hampstead Theatre. Both plays subsequently ran at New York's Manhattan Theatre Club and *The Memory of Water* has been produced all over the world. Her third play, *Ancient Lights*, was produced at Hampstead Theatre in December 2000. She has written several radio plays, most recently the award-winning *Five Kinds of Silence*, which she adapted for the stage and which was presented at the Lyric, Hammersmith in 2000. Her screen adaptation of *The Memory of Water* was released in spring 2002 under the title *Before You Go*.

Mappa Mundi premiered at the Cottesloe, Royal National Theatre, London, on 24 October 2002. The cast was as follows:

Jack	Ian Holm
Michael, *his son*	Tim McInnerny
Anna, *his daughter*	Lia Williams
Father Ryan	James Hayes
Sholto, *Anna's fiancé*	Patrick Robinson
Portia, *Sholto's mother*	Alibe Parsons
Dancers	Cody Choi
	Juliet Codlin
	Gerrard Martin
	Benny Maslov
	Lorena Randi
	Supple

Director Bill Alexander
Designer Ruari Murchison
Music Director Paul Pyant
Composer Jonathan Goldstein
Choreographer Arthur Pita
Sound Designer David Tinson

Mappa Mundi

Shelagh Stephenson

Methuen Drama

Published by Methuen Drama

1 3 5 7 9 10 8 6 4 2

First published in 2002 by
Methuen Publishing Limited

Copyright © Shelagh Stephenson 2002

Shelagh Stephenson has asserted her right under the Copyright, Designs
and Patents Act, 1988, to be identified as the author of this work.

A CIP catalogue record is available from the British Library

ISBN 0 413 77302 7

Typeset by SX Composing DTP, Rayleigh, Essex
Printed and bound in Great Britain by
Cox & Wyman Ltd, Reading, Berkshire

Caution

For Eoin

Act One

Lights and music blaze up at the same moment. A garden at night, present day. A backdrop of grainy, blown up family photographs, from various dates in the late nineteenth and twentieth centuries. Also, a fantastical eighteenth century map showing mermaids and dancing girls, waterfalls and imaginary beasts. Wild fiddle music plays, African drums, Northumbrian pipes. A group of dancers and a band burst onto the stage. The music is at once familiar and strange, a mix of English traditional, Irish, African, Asian, Eastern. The troupe of dancers are Black, Asian and Caucasian, and their dance is as strange and as revelatory as the music: English rapper sword dancing, meets African tribal, meets traditional Indian dance meets something other. It's leaping and vigorous, joyful, passionate, and utterly itself. The music whirls faster, the dancers swoop and leap. The dance and music should be compelling enough to last at least five minutes. The dancers whirl themselves into exhaustion, and as the music fades they throw themselves onto the ground, exhilarated and prostrated. From the shadows emerges **Sholto***, a black lawyer in his late thirties, applauding.*

Sholto   It's going to be brilliant, guys. They're going to love it. Thank you. So when you've all got your breath back, it's down the pub and drinks are on me . . .

Blackout.

Lights up on same garden in high summer. Sunlight filtering through trees. Birds, the sound of distant lawnmowers. The World Service plays on a portable radio. ('This is Carmen Rodriguez, BBC World Service, Havana, John Taylor, BBC World Service, Warsaw, Moses Umbekwe, BBC World Service, Johannesburg, etc., etc.) Laughter and the hum of conversation can be heard, off. An elderly man, **Jack***, wakes from a slumber in a hammock.*

Jack   Hello . . . ?

He struggles to get out of the hammock, without success.

Michael . . . ?

He waits. Nobody comes.

Michael!

Nobody comes.

Help!

Nobody comes.

Somebody get me out of this fucking thing!

His son **Michael**, *forties, comes out.*

Michael Have a nice kip?

He turns off the radio.

Jack I was listening to that.

Michael You were asleep.

Jack Where's Anna?

Michael You were shouting for me.

Jack I was shouting for Anna.

Michael OK. I'll piss off then.

His sister, **Anna**, *comes out, four years younger than him, brisk and beautiful.*

Anna Who put him in that hammock?

Michael I never touched him . . .

Jack I'm stuck in the bloody thing.

Michael Why didn't you say?

They help him out.

Anna Come on. Where would you like to go? Sun or shade?

Jack Go on, shove me in the sun, might as well get a melanoma on top of everything else.

Anna I'll put you in the shade.

She sits him down.

Jack   You're a good girl. The best.

Anna   Yes, Dad.

Jack (*to* **Michael**)   You said you'd bring me a whisky.

Anna   He did. You drank it.

Jack   Don't start this lark. Telling me I don't know what's going on.

Michael *picks up a half-empty tumbler from the ground.*

Michael   Here's your glass. You didn't finish it.

Jack *takes the glass, puzzled.*

Jack   Is that mine?

Anna   Yes.

Jack   It's these drugs they've got me on.

Anna   That's probably it.

Jack   I'm all at sixes and sevens.

He sips the whisky, shakily. Silence. He pats **Anna***'s hand.*

Jack   I never had a moment's trouble with this one. Never lost a wink of sleep. She didn't even do adolescent sulking.

Michael   Shall we have her beatified, what d'you think?

Jack   You made up for it though.

Anna   Dad –

Jack   Forest.

Michael   Sorry?

Jack   What?

Anna   Are you sure you don't want to come inside for a lie-down, Dad?

Jack   Forest. What does it mean?

Anna *and* **Michael** *exchange a look.*

Michael   It's a kind of . . . wood thing. Trees. Are you all right?

Anna   Have you had your other tablet?

Jack   It's nothing to do with trees. That's not the original meaning of the word at all.

Anna   Isn't it?

Jack   It means a deer park. A place where deer were kept. Some forests had no trees at all.

Anna   Goodness. I never knew that.

Michael   You should write a book, Dad. Jack Armstrong's book of arcane information that won't change your life.

Jack   A fact's always a good thing. It can never be a bad thing. D'you agree?

She looks at her watch.

Anna   Why don't you come inside, Dad?

Jack   It might not please you, but it's indisputable. You can't argue with a fact.

Anna   D'you remember if you took your other tab –

Jack   Here's another thing. Leave any piece of land untouched, it'll revert to woodland within fifty years. That's another fact.

Michael   What about the desert?

Jack   The desert's a different kettle of fish.

Michael   What about Antarctica?

Anna   Michael.

Jack   I'm talking about England. I don't know anything about Antarctica. Acorns dropped by jays, sycamore seedlings. Knock down this house, leave well alone, and the woods will reclaim it. Fact.

Michael   So how does that make you feel?

Jack   Irrelevant.

Anna *looks at her watch again, agitated.*

Anna   A hundred and fifty glasses. D'you think that'll be enough? They were supposed to arrive two hours ago.

Jack   Got a cigarette?

Anna   I thought you'd stopped? You told me you'd stopped.

Jack   What difference does it make at my age?

Michael *hands him a cigarette, lights it for him.*

Anna   Are you smoking in your flat?

Jack   No.

Anna   Oh, for God's sake.

Jack   I've just said I'm not.

Michael   Leave him alone. He has the occasional fag, so what?

Anna   Will you stop siding with him? It's my bloody house that'll go up in flames if he leaves one down the side of the sofa again –

Michael   Oh, excuse me, here's me thinking it's his health you're worried about, when obviously it's just your furniture –

Anna   Look –

Jack   Is the priest –

Anna   It's not actually funny, Michael –

Michael   Am I laughing?

Anna   It's not laughing, it's this oh, it's all a bit of a joke thing. Well can I just point out that it's not, and did you tell the florists to fuck off this morning because someone did?

Michael   I never spoke to the bloody florist –

Jack   Is anybody listening to me?

Anna   Sorry, Dad, yes, what?

Jack   Is Father Ryan still there?

Anna   Why don't you come in and see him? You can talk to him while I make some phone calls –

Jack   What's he doing here anyway?

Anna   He just, you know, dropped in.

Jack   Dropped in, my arse. He wants to give me the last rites.

Michael   Of course he doesn't.

Anna   Why would he want to do that?

Jack   Hah!

Anna   He called in to see how you were, that's all.

Jack   Bloody ghouls. Hanging around death beds waiting to filch your soul.

Michael   Maybe they're on commission.

Jack   Well they're not having mine.

Anna   You're not on your deathbed.

Jack   He doesn't know that.

Michael   Do many people die in hammocks, d'you think?

Jack   They trawl the neighbourhood in search of the nearly dead. Like body snatchers.

Anna   He's here to talk to Sholto and me about the wedding. You said you wanted religion in the ceremony so he's going to do a blessing. We're doing it to make you happy. That's what he's doing here. OK?

Jack   'Dear Lord and Father of Mankind, Forgive our Foolish Ways.'

Michael   What?

Jack   That's a good one. (*Sings.*) 'Speak through the earth quake, wind and fire –'

Anna   We're not having hymns, Dad. Sholto's arranged for a band –

Jack   Sholto. What a stupid name.

Anna   If you say that once more –

Jack   Sholto. He's probably from one of them cargo cults, is he?

Anna   That's Polynesia, Dad. He comes from Leicestershire.

Jack   I mean originally. Before they came over here.

Michael   They don't have cargo cults in the West Indies.

Jack   They do, they worship Prince Philip. Big fella belong Missis Quinn.

Michael   That's bloody Polynesia, we've just told you.

Jack   All right, all right, no need to shout.

Anna   If you start this in front of Sholto and his mother –

Michael   We'll have to put you in a home.

Jack   You'd like that.

Michael   A dog's home.

A priest in his fifties comes out, glass in hand.

Father Ryan   Jack, how are you?

Jack   Fine.

He makes a gurgling sound, and his head drops to his chest. They stare at him.

Anna   Dad?

Father Ryan   Jack?

Michael   Dad, are you all right?

Anna *goes to him, lifts his head.*

Anna   He's not breathing . . . Dad? He's stopped breathing –

Michael *comes over.*

Michael   Dad? Jesus, he's –

Father Ryan *takes over.*

Father Ryan   Jack, can you hear me?

Suddenly **Jack** *jerks his head.*

Jack   Just testing.

Michael   You bastard.

Anna   That was horrible –

Jack   I didn't notice much wailing and gnashing of teeth. You didn't sound very grief-stricken.

Father Ryan   That was a bit of a mean trick now, Jack –

Jack   What d'you want anyway?

Father Ryan   Ah, come on, Jack, can I not make a social call? I came to see how you're settling in –

Anna   Dad, that was a really cruel thing to do.

Jack   Fine. I've settled in fine. Why wouldn't I?

Father Ryan   Sure I only thought –

Jack   A granny flat. That's what it's called, isn't it? All mod cons. A deep fat fryer. Electric.

Father Ryan   They're great things those fryers.

Anna   We didn't want –

Michael   After the last time –

Father Ryan   No –

Jack   It was an electrical fault. I didn't leave the gas on –

Father Ryan   Anyway, you escaped in one piece and that's all that matters, Jack.

Jack   Shame about the house.

Father Ryan   Yes.

A beat.

Father Ryan   Have you thought about calling in to mass one these days, Jack?

Jack   No. (*To* **Michael** *and* **Anna**.) I told you. I knew he was angling for something.

Father Ryan   Not at all, not at all. How's the book I lent you?

Jack   Not helpful.

Father Ryan   I'm sorry about that. What couldn't you get on with?

Jack   At one point I threw the bloody thing at the wall I was so frustrated. If that's the way the world is I've been barking up the wrong tree. You don't know if you're coming or going. Up's down, down's up, sometimes it's this, sometimes it's that, sometimes it's both at the same time, but it depends how you look at it. Or *if* you look at it. Is it dead or alive, no it's both.

Father Ryan (*to* **Michael** *and* **Anna**)   *The Tao of Physics.*

Michael   My God, Dad's gone New Age. Shall we get you some crystals and a nose flute?

Anna   I'm very impressed.

Jack   It's not New Age. It's not helpful either.

Michael   What sort of help were you looking for, Dad?

Jack   I had no idea about any of this stuff. Why didn't someone tell me earlier in my life when I could have got to grips with it a bit?

Michael   So you got into it then? I'm astonished.

Jack   It's keeping me awake at night.

Father Ryan   I'm sorry. Actually, Jack, I didn't come to grill you on your reading habits, I only came to make the final arrangements for the wedding –

Jack   A light buffet, nothing too heavy.

Anna   Dad, don't worry about the food, it'll be fine, there'll be something you can eat.

Jack   Little sandwiches. A scone maybe.

Anna   OK, OK, we'll make sure there's some scones, I'll phone the bakers and order scones –

Jack   No, no, don't put yourself out. I'll force down a Thai fishcake if I have to.

Anna   Jesus Christ, Dad, I'm trying to organise a wedding for a hundred people, have you any idea how difficult that is without having to constantly think about your weird dietary whims –

Jack   I said a scone, what's weird about a scone –

Anna   Because we're not having scones, it's not that sort of do, but if you want scones, fine, I'll get them –

Jack   I'm talking about an ideal here. In an ideal world there would be scones –

Michael   We'll get you some fucking scones, OK?

Anna   Michael.

Jack (*to* **Father Ryan**)   You see what I have to put up with?

Father Ryan (*desperately*)   Anna's been giving me a look at your maps, Jack. That's a great collection you've got there. I don't remember seeing them in the old place.

Jack   Kept them under lock and key. But there's burglar alarms and whatnot here, so I can have them on display. That's all I worried about when the house went up. My maps and my papers. A few photographs. Didn't care about the rest.

Father Ryan   It's amazing you had the presence of mind to rescue them, given the chaos.

Jack   Of course I had the presence of mind, I'm not senile.

Father Ryan   Anyway, you got out, Jack, that's the thing.

Jack   I miss it. I dream I'm at home again, in my own bed, and when I wake up I'm not. I'm in a granny flat.

Father Ryan   Plenty of space though, Jack.

Jack   'The Day Thou Gavest Lord is Ended.' That's another one.

Anna   Not for a wedding, Dad.

Jack   I'm just saying.

Anna   What?

Jack   It's a nice hymn.

Michael   But not at a wedding.

Jack   I never said that.

Michael   So why bring it up?

Father Ryan   But isn't it a great little flat you have here, Jack? You're lucky Anna's got such a marvellous place, the size of it and all. Isn't it great she's done so well –

Jack (*indicating* **Michael**)   I wish *he'd* get a proper job –

Michael It is a proper job –

Jack It's insecure.

Anna Don't start, Dad –

Her mobile rings.

Michael There's no such thing as a secure job any more.

Anna (*into phone*) Hello?

Jack Your sister managed it.

Michael I don't want to be a lawyer.

Anna (*into phone*) Champagne flutes, that's right.

Jack Look at this place. Look at the size of it. And what have you got? A bedsit off the Holloway Road.

Michael It's not a bedsit.

Anna (*into phone*) . . . No, not a funeral, who drinks champagne at a funeral? It's a wedding . . . that's OK . . . so when will they arrive?

Michael And it's nowhere near Holloway Road, that was in nineteen seventy-nine –

Anna (*into phone*) OK, thanks, bye.

She clicks off the phone.

Jack You have me worried sick, that's all –

Michael I've been doing it for twenty years, Dad, get over it.

Jack If every actor died tomorrow, you know what? No one would notice.

Michael Thanks, Dad. Thanks for wishing me dead.

Jack You see? He takes the bait every time.

Anna Look, I'm getting married, I've got a lot on my plate and I'm tense. Has anyone noticed that? Maybe you think these things just come together by sleight of hand, but actually they don't and all either of you've done is loll about and occasionally open another bottle of wine –

Jack   I never knew I was supposed to do anything –

Anna   Not you, Dad –

Michael   Oh I see, what exactly is it you require? Should I be sewing sequins on your frock? Embroidering the ritual bridal tampons?

Jack   Watch your mouth, you.

Anna   I want sweetness and joy and light, I want us to be pleasant and polite and considerate to each other –

Michael   We've never managed it in forty-five years, why should we start now?

Anna   Because I'm trying to organise a wedding and I'm attempting to stay CALM! OK?

Michael   OK, OK. Why didn't you just nip into a registry office and get married, why d'you have to have all this palaver –

Anna   Because I want palaver, all right?

Jack   I made a passing comment about actors, that's all –

Father Ryan   I think you're being a bit harsh about them, Jack. Where would we be without the films?

Jack   Exactly where I am now. I haven't been to the cinema since nineteen sixty-two.

Father Ryan   I'm bit of a Kevin Spacey fan, myself.

Jack   Last time I said actors served no useful purpose, he called me a cunt.

Anna   Will you stop it!

Jack   Well, he did.

Michael   Well, you are.

Anna   For goodness sake! Father Ryan's here.

Father Ryan   Ah, don't mind me.

Jack   If a policeman called you a cunt, you could sue him. But with an actor, it's water off a duck's back. It's cunt this and cunt that all the time in the theatre. Apparently. They mean it affectionately. So he says.

Michael   Sorry about this Father Ryan.

Jack   Causing a bit of a scene am I?

Anna   Just behave, will you?

Jack   Cunt. If you say it enough, it takes the sting off it.

Anna   Will you stop it, right now. I'm so sorry, Father, this is – I mean he's – he doesn't usually swear – not like this –

Father Ryan   You were saying about the maps, Jack –

Anna   Yes, the maps, let's get back to the maps, can we –

Jack   Try it, go on. Cunt.

Father Ryan   They must be very valuable.

Jack   It's just a word, isn't it? One little word. Cunt. But it goes off like an atom bomb.

Anna   Dad if you don't stop this I seriously am going to have you put in a home. You'll have to wear a plastic bib and incontinence pants and spend all day with old women with beards that you can't stand, and believe me, you won't like it. But it'll serve you right.

Jack   Haven't you got things to do? I thought you had glasses to count. Scones to order.

She goes out, exasperated.

I don't know what's got into her. Very touchy.

Michael   Have you got it out of your system now, Dad, or is there a risk you might pipe up with the 'C' word during the wedding ceremony?

Jack   You started it.

Michael   Oh, for God's sake –

Father Ryan   I particularly liked the map with the --

Jack   Eighteenth century, those maps are, which means they're copper engravings, right?

Father Ryan   I see.

Jack   No you don't.

Father Ryan   You're right, I don't.

Jack   They're not steel engravings. Not stone lithographs. That was nineteenth century. Around eighteen twenty they started using steel. You can make more copies with it because it's hard, it lasts longer. You don't want to get me going on chromo-lithography.

Father Ryan   Do I not?

Michael   Believe me, you don't. Nothing the Inquisition did compares with the sheer offensiveness of a chromo-lithograph.

Jack   Flat, mass produced, no depth. You get the detail but not the texture. You don't get the feel you get with copper. Copper's a soft metal, easier to engrave, but it wears down when you take a lot of imprints. You can't make as many good copies. They get a bit woolly over the years. That's what I like about them, they're all a bit different.

Michael   They were done by a relative of ours.

Father Ryan   Yes, Anna told me.

Jack   So he's family. He's who I am. If I touch those maps under the glass I'm touching what he touched. His fingerprints, his cells. And they'd be my cells as well. Have I got the biology right?

Michael   No.

Jack   Mind you I'm going back a bit. Seventeen thirty-eight he was born. It doesn't seem that long ago anymore. Time's telescoping now. My mother was born in eighteen ninety-three. A whole century seems embraceable these days, I can hold it in my hand. It's not history anymore, I can reach out and touch it.

Father Ryan   When I was a tiny boy, I sat on the lap of a very old woman, she must have been going on a hundred, and she told me that when she was a child she'd sat on the lap of a very old man who'd been a page at the court of Marie Antoinette. Doesn't that make you think?

Michael   She was probably lying.

Father Ryan   Not at all. Three hands stretched out across the years, that's all it is. The past's just a fingertip away.

Jack   I traced the family tree. Thomas Goode was the map maker. Goode by name and good by nature.

Michael   Well, there's one characteristic you didn't inherit.

Jack (*suddenly sharp*)   Meaning?

Michael   It was a joke, it was joke, OK? Anyway, he owned slave plantations, he wasn't that good.

Jack   You can't judge the past by the present. There was more to him than his mistakes. He built a town hall. Two local hospitals –

Michael   Off the back of slave owning –

Jack   Why are you upsetting me like this?

Michael   Because it's true.

Jack   I know it's bloody true, what d'you want me to do about it? It was two hundred years ago.

Father Ryan   Ah, come on now, if we keep going back and blaming like this we'll never be done, will we. Everyone got screwed by someone –

Jack   He mapped his own estates, Thomas Goode. They're very fine, if a little exaggerated.

Father Ryan   In what sense?

Jack   Well, he made them a bit bigger than they actually were. What's there on the maps doesn't square with what's there in the records.

Michael   He was a fraudulent, slave owning, serial adulterer. Why are you so desperate to be his relative. Is it a class thing? Is it that little frisson of blue blood that gets you in a lather?

Jack (*to* **Ryan**)   I've heard all this before. They think he was influenced by a French map maker called John Roche.

Michael   And we're not actually direct descendants, Dad, we're the bastard line. Like half the county, probably. He was a notorious womaniser.

Jack   So? I was always told we had something to do with a famous map maker somewhere way back. I liked that. I used to look at an old atlas in Newcastle Central Library. *The World Mercator*. Mercator. What a word. Even the shape of it on the page. The strangeness of it.

Father Ryan   What does it actually mean?

Jack   I thought it was a scientific term, I never knew it was a person. It sounded mysterious and impenetrable to me, like a secret code.

Father Ryan   So, the one I noticed, with the gold leaf and dancing girls and camels. Is that the same man?

Jack   They think so.

Father Ryan   And it's a map of where?

Jack   Somewhere in the Middle East he never went to. He probably copied it. It's in a bad state but I paid over the odds for it because I liked it, even though it's falling to bits.

Father Ryan   Why?

Jack   Why what?

Father Ryan   Did you like it so much.

Jack   It just took my fancy. No particular reason.

Father Ryan   It must have taken you a fair old amount of time tracking down the family tree.

Jack   It took years. There's still a few gaps. Anna swears we've got an African in there somewhere –

Father Ryan   Oh that's very exotic. My mother had the idea we were a bit racy because her grandmother came from Crossmaglen.

Michael   She's been digging around in the family swamp and come up with someone named Dido. Thomas Goode's bit on the side.

Father Ryan   And how d'you know she was black?

Michael   We've only Anna's word for it. They're on divergent paths: Dad's trying to prove he's a direct descendant of John Bull, Chaucer and Robin Hood, and she's trying to prove she's genetically connected to Martin Luther King, Sidney Poitier and Nelson Mandela. Mind you, I can see her point.

Jack   I've looked in the mirror and I can't see it personally. I've never even had a suntan.

Michael   He's just thrilled he can hold his head up in Brixton, aren't you, Dad? He's thinking of getting in touch with his inner rap artist.

Anna *comes out with* **Sholto**.

Anna   Michael? Phone. Quick. It's probably your agent.

Michael   Fuck off.

He goes.

Anna   Sorry everyone's so foul-mouthed, Father. It's the strain.

Father Ryan   They're all at the swearing these days. I went to give an old woman the last rites yesterday and she only told me to eff off. Eighty-three years old she was. They get it off the television.

Sholto   I'm going to collect my mum from the station, d'you want to come, Jack?

Anna   Yes, why don't you go with Sholto, Dad?

Jack   Why?

Anna   Change of scenery.

Jack   Are you coming?

Anna   I've got too much to do.

Jack   No. No thanks.

Anna   Go on, it's an outing.

Jack   I don't want to go to the station.

Sholto   I can put the roof down on the car.

Jack   No, I don't want to come.

Anna   Go on, Dad, go for the ride.

Jack   Go for the ride? For Christ's sake, how old d'you think I am? I've been in a bloody car before –

Anna   All right, all right, don't, forget it, he doesn't want to come Sholto –

Jack   Mind you, I hardly ever get out these days.

Sholto   So are you coming or not?

Jack   No, I think I'll stay.

Sholto   OK, I'll see you later –

Jack   Will you be going through the car wash?

Sholto   I hadn't planned to.

Jack   I wouldn't mind a go of the car wash. The one you drive through.

Sholto   OK, well, I mean if you want to –

Jack   All right then, I'll come. If we can go through the car wash.

Anna   Jesus Christ.

Jack   I asked Michael to take me through the other day and he refused point blank.

He gets up.

I have a fantasy that I'll drive through a car wash one day and come out the other side in an alternative reality.

Father Ryan   I see . . .

Jack   D'you never have that hope?

Father Ryan   Not with a car wash, no.

Sholto *takes his arm.*

Sholto   Come on, Jack, give me your arm –

Jack   I can manage . . .

He shrugs **Sholto** *off.*

Father Ryan   Take care now, Jack. And if you ever feel like coming to mass –

Jack (*under his breath*)   Ah, bugger off.

They go out. **Anna** *looks at* **Father Ryan**.

Anna   Sorry.

Father Ryan   Eff off, bugger off, that's all I get these days. I'm used to it.

Anna   Disinhibited, the doctor calls it.

Father Ryan   How long has he got?

Anna   A couple of months. Three maybe.

Father Ryan   Does he know that?

Anna   No.

Father Ryan   He knows something.

Anna   Maybe if you've lived inside your body for seventy odd years, you get an inkling of something. Some tectonic shift inside you. It doesn't mean he knows objectively, that he's dying. And I'm not about to ruin whatever time he has left. What's the point? Anyway, it's not my job to tell him.

Father Ryan   Is it your job to withhold it from him?

Anna   He's relatively happy, and I don't see any reason to make him fearful.

Father Ryan   Because that would be difficult for you to deal with?

Anna   No, because it would be difficult for him to deal with.

Father Ryan   How do you know?

Anna   All right then, it would be difficult for all of us, and I don't want, I've got too much, I mean –

Father Ryan   Sorry, sorry, I know.

Anna   There's a present being delivered for him, and it's a surprise, so we had to get him out of the house.

Father Ryan   It's not his birthday, is it?

Anna   No, that's December, but we thought . . . well, he probably won't.. I mean we hope to God he will be but . . .

Father Ryan   Right, right.

Pause.

Must be a big present.

Anna   It was Michael's idea. The thing is, he's sort of obsessed with this family tree thing at the moment. Who he is, where he's come from.

Father Ryan   He's trying to work it out before he goes. It's an age thing. Lots of people do it. They start to identify with the dead more than the living.

Anna   He's always felt a bit dislocated. He never really had a family to anchor him. Brought up by someone he called an aunt but she wasn't really. I don't think they were related at all. She was just some family friend. Did he ever tell you that?

Father Ryan   He told me once he felt cut adrift. Maybe that's what he meant. I couldn't work it out at the time. Drink had been taken, you know. (*He looks at his watch.*) Anyway, I'd better get going.

He hesitates.

Father Ryan   He's being very good about the wedding.

Anna   What d'you mean, good?

Father Ryan   Sholto being of a different . . . you know. Although maybe the black ancestor's changed his views a bit.

Anna   Oh he told you did he? What did he say?

Father Ryan   He said he can't see it himself.

Anna   No. He's decided not to believe it.

Father Ryan   He wouldn't. Jack's a great one for banging on about being English. Whatever that means.

Anna   Sholto's English. He was born in Market Harborough.

Father Ryan   It took your father years before he stopped greeting me with, 'Top of the morning begorrah to be sure.' He still does it sometimes.

Anna   Oh God, I'm so sorry.

Father Ryan   In a terrible accent. Desperate.

Anna   He's not being that good about Sholto and me actually. He just comes at it obliquely. 'It's the children I'll feel sorry for, neither one thing nor the other. Poor little half-castes.' That's what he came out with the other day.

Father Ryan   He has his redeeming features.

Anna   Such as?

Father Ryan   The swearing and what have you. It's just guff, it's self protection –

Michael *comes back.*

Michael   I've been offered a film!

Anna   Have you? When?

Michael   Well, not offered.

Father Ryan   I love that Kevin Spacey. D'you know the one I mean?

Michael   It probably won't work out.

Anna   Will you have to go back to London?

Michael   Well, at some point. I told him things were a bit tricky at the moment.

Father Ryan   Will Kevin Spacey be in it?

Michael   Not as far as I know.

Father Ryan   That's a shame. What about the other Kevin. Cosgrove is it?

Michael   Costner. No, he's not in it either. Is it the name Kevin that attracts you?

Father Ryan   Not at all. I'm also a great fan of Felicity Kendal.

Michael   I think you're out of luck there as well.

Anna   If we can just get the wedding out of the way. Maybe you could get home for a few days after that.

Michael   It's like waiting for someone to give birth. When's it due? Could be any time now. Except we're waiting for a death day, not a birthday.

Father Ryan   You haven't talked to him about it at all?

Michael   We don't really have that sort of conversation. He tells me interesting facts and I take the piss. I tell him what I'm up to and he takes the piss.

Father Ryan   Maybe you should. Have the conversation.

Michael   Actually, I've no idea who Dad is. I mean, I know what he's like, but I don't know who he is.

Anna   You don't. You don't know your parents except as your parents. But on some level you recognise every single cell of them. Every look, every gesture, every word not said. It kills you.

Father Ryan   But try and talk to him if you can, both of you.

Michael   It's not that easy.

Father Ryan   I never said it was. But if you don't, he'll be dead, and you'll never know any more about him than you do now. And first you'll feel nostalgic, and then you'll start making him up. You'll invent a version of him, like a comfort blanket, and it'll be bollocks, excuse my French. And a person deserves more than that. Anyway, I'd better get going –

Anna   I'll see you out –

Father Ryan   No, no, stay here. I'll call in tomorrow, to see how things are shaping up.

He goes.

Michael   Try and talk to him. Christ.

Anna   Maybe he's right.

Michael   Of course he's right. But has he ever tried to have a conversation with Dad? And incidentally, I never called him a cunt.

Anna   You did. I heard you.

Michael   Under my breath.

Anna   He's got very acute hearing. Like a bat. He only pretends to be deaf.

Michael *lights up a cigarette.*

Michael   Well he's a pain. With me anyway. You know he is. You, on the other hand, could admit to serial killing and he'd still be comparing you to Saint Berna-fucking-dette.

Pause.

Anna   What's the film about?

Michael   I'm only pencilled in.

Anna   So?

Michael   It's a mockney gangster caper set in Clerkenwell.

Anna   A client of mine's just bought a loft in Clerkenwell –

Michael   I'll be playing a drugs dealer with a Weimaraner who has a cache of diamonds up its arse. Or maybe I have. Anyway someone has. And it all goes horribly wrong. Except not very, because it's a) British and b) a caper, so it's ironic you see and all the psychopaths love their old mums really. I'm depressed just thinking about it.

Anna   But that's good. It's a film.

Michael The director's an old Etonian with Hank Marvin glasses who calls everyone mate.

Anna I bet it's not as bad as you're making out.

Michael Oh it is. It's worse. But you know. Mortgage. Bread on table. Stuff. And on and on till the bitter end, and my obituary says he was in some bad films and some worse commercials but luckily most of the latter were in German. That's if I get an obituary. God, I could shoot myself.

Pause.

By the way. The stuff about hymns and I-think-I-might-manage-a-scone. He's not actually talking about the wedding.

Anna Sorry?

Michael Dad. He's not talking about the wedding when he brings that stuff up.

Anna So what is he talking about?

Michael His funeral.

Anna No he's not, don't be stupid.

Michael He is. He's trying to tell us what he wants at his funeral without actually telling us.

Anna But he doesn't know he's dying.

Michael Of course he fucking does.

Anna Figuratively. He doesn't know the reality of it.

Michael How d'you know he doesn't know?

Anna Because I know him better than you do.

Michael How do you know?

Anna Because I spend more time with him.

Michael And he's said, 'Hey d'you know what, I'm not dying,' has he?

Anna   He talks about next year. He talks about getting a dog. People who know they're dying don't get dogs.

Michael   Actually, they do. It's very common.

Anna   Anyway, I'm not getting him one. Who'd walk it?

Michael   Maybe you could get him a hamster. Or a stick insect. They don't last long. That way you wouldn't be left with it.

Anna   D'you really feel like shooting yourself?

Michael   I feel I'm hurtling towards old age and decrepitude and death. Sometimes I lie in bed staring at the ceiling and imagine all the people who've died in that room and what does it all mean anyway.

Anna   You're only forty-five.

Michael   I have varicose veins. They disgust me. I lie in bed at night and wish I was a Christian. Or a Buddhist. A Seventh Day Adventist. Anything to fill the void.

Anna   You're lonely. You'll meet someone and everything will change.

Michael   Acting used to do it for me. Can you believe that? It used to give my life meaning. And now it doesn't because it's dawned on me that I don't do the sort of work that gives anything any kind of meaning. Hence the desire to shoot myself in the head.

Anna   Sometimes when I feel a bit low, I try cutting down on wheat –

Michael   And when Dad blahs on about the uselessness of actors I want to defend myself and I can't because all the work I do is shite and completely indefensible.

Anna   It's not. You're exaggerating. And anyway it earns you money. There are worse ways of making a living.

Michael   Am I depressing you?

Anna   A bit.

Pause.

Anna   When are we going to give him the present?

Michael   I don't know. Tomorrow night?

He looks at his watch.

Michael   Half three. Is that all it is? What is it about weddings, imminent death and the possibility of being in another crap film that makes you desperate for alcohol?

Lights down. Lights up on same garden, night.

Sholto *is practising his wedding speech, paper and pencil in hand, glass of wine on the table.*

Sholto   Ladies and Gentlemen . . .

Pause. He thinks about it.

Sholto   Hi everyone. I've never made a speech in public that wasn't devoted to legal precedent, plea bargaining, or getting my client off the hook, so you'll have to forgive the odd lapse into legalese. On second thoughts, Anna 'll never forgive me, so can I just say now that she's the most fantastic –

Anna *comes out with a joint.*

Anna   D'you want some of this?

Sholto   I'm trying to write my speech.

Anna   I was trying to write mine but I've given up. Are you sure you don't want some of this?

Sholto   No thanks. Are you sure you should?

Anna   There's no tobacco in it. And it certainly puts things in perspective.

Sholto   How?

Anna   I was trying to sort out wine lists and food deliveries and who hadn't replied yet. Three puffs of this and I couldn't give a fuck.

He takes the joint from her, takes a drag, and coughs. He hands it back.

Sholto   I can't do it anymore. Too old.

Anna   Are you glad you're marrying me?

Sholto   Are you glad you're marrying me?

Anna   I just said that.

Sholto   Of course I'm glad.

Anna   Who else would have either of us?

Sholto   You getting nervous again?

Anna   No.

Sholto   You're not going to run away again?

Anna   No.

Sholto   A whole lifetime. That's quite a big commitment. Are you sure you can face it?

Anna   I can if you can.

He takes the joint again and has another drag. Suppresses a cough.

Sholto   You never really explained to me. Why you, you know.

Anna   Fucked off for three weeks?

Sholto   You never explained it properly. You were frightened, you had cold feet, you were worried about . . . What? What were you worried about?

Anna   It's a big thing. My whole life sewn up. No alternatives. No get outs.

Sholto   You're not convincing me.

Anna   I was frightened. You're right, I was frightened. Not because I didn't love you. That wasn't it.

Sholto   Whatever it was it nearly killed me.

Anna   I know. I'm sorry. Why are we doing this now?

Sholto   Clearing the air before the big day. Let's-not-go-to-the-altar-with-something-unresolved and all that.

Anna   It's because I didn't want to watch you die.

Sholto   What?

Anna   I looked at you one day, and I was just thinking how much I loved you when it suddenly dawned on me that if I married you, I'd be the one at your death bed.

Sholto   I'm not going to die.

Anna   Of course you are.

Sholto   Not for ages.

Anna   I didn't mean it was imminent, it's just that I saw the end, and I ran away from it, because it was too much to bear. It seemed like such a huge responsibility.

Sholto   You might die first. I might be at your death bed.

Anna   I know, but I didn't think of that then. I just looked at you and knew that one day, I'd be looking at your face and you'd be dead. And I thought that if I didn't marry you, I wouldn't have to do that.

Sholto   Most people think of marriage as a shared life. You think of it as a shared death –

Anna   No, I think it's a life as well, it's just that death comes into it eventually, and that's what you're taking on when you take on the life. D'you see?

Sholto   Can I just say that that's not a balanced way of looking at the world?

Anna   Why d'you think I never explained it properly? I was too embarrassed. That's why I came back. I realised I was being ridiculous –

Suddenly **Jack** *shoots onto the stage in an electric wheelchair.* **Anna** *jumps out of the way.*

Anna   Jesus Christ!

Jack   You can get up a hell of a speed on this thing.

Sholto   I thought you said you never wanted to use it Jack?

Jack   I didn't realise what it was capable of –

He shoots forwards and backwards, almost crashing into **Sholto**.

Sholto   OK, OK, slow down –

Anna *stubs out the joint.*

Anna   We were just going in. It's getting cold.

Jack   D'you know Schrodinger's cat?

Anna   Whose cat?

Jack   It's in one of those books Father Ryan lent me. The cat in the box thing.

Sholto   You know, is it alive or is it dead, or is it both.

Anna   What?

Jack   I don't think that's quite it.

Sholto   Is it not?

Jack   There's a cat in a box with an atom, which may, or may not, at some point, decay, breaking a phial of poison which will kill the cat –

Anna   Dad, what are you getting at?

Jack   It was in this book. It's scientific fact. You can't argue with a fact.

Sholto   Actually, I think it's more of a metaphor.

Jack   Anyway, the cat's in the box. Locked in. Is it alive or dead?

Anna   I haven't a clue.

Sholto   It's neither.

Jack   Correct.

Anna   How d'you know these things Sholto?

Jack   It's neither dead nor alive. It's in some indeterminate state until someone looks in the box to find out what's happening. But there's two ways of looking at this. Either there's no cat, dead or alive, until you open the box and look at it. Or both states are real: there's a dead cat and a live one, but they exist in different worlds. So you can only observe one at a time.

Anna   And your point is?

Jack   You see what's thrown me here is this: is there another version of everything, that's almost the same but a bit different? Another version of me for instance? Where I made some different choices along the way, and I'm living a different life?

Anna   No, of course there isn't.

Jack   But there might be.

Sholto   Even if there is, it doesn't mean anything without consciousness does it? I mean, you can only live one life. You can't slip through some time membrane and experience another one.

Anna   I don't think these books are doing you any good, do you, Dad?

Jack   It's bloody odd though. What if there is another version of me in some parallel universe. Or hundreds even. A me who made different choices.

Sholto   Why d'you want to have made different choices?

Jack   Did I say that?

Sholto   D'you wish you had, is that it?

Jack   That's not what I said. Why would I want to have made different choices?

Sholto   I don't know. Doesn't everybody wish that a bit?

Jack   Do they?

Sholto   I do. I think I should have followed my heart and been a dancer instead of following my desire for respectability and becoming a lawyer. On the other hand I probably wasn't good enough to dance so maybe it worked out for the best. But you always wonder. What if. What if.

Jack   I did the best I could.

Anna   Of course you did, Dad –

Jack   I never deliberately harmed anyone –

Anna   Nobody's suggesting that.

Jack   When I was at school science was test tubes and Bunsen burners. No-one said anything about particles being waves and cats in boxes. And now it's too late. I'll never grasp it.

Anna   It doesn't matter, Dad.

Jack   I've spent my entire life not knowing the fundamentals.

Anna   And it hasn't harmed you, has it?

Jack   I don't know. I'm tired. That's the problem, I'm tired. I'm too old to learn new things. It's depressing me. It's been there all the time and I never knew.

Anna   I don't think you should worry about it, Dad, honestly. Why don't you read some of the other books Father Ryan gave you?

Jack   *Jesus Christ: The Man Behind the Myth. The Little Book of Buddhist Meditation*, two Dick Francis novels and *Bikram Yoga* *for the Over Seventies.* You see why I went for the physics. Have you got a cigarette?

Anna   You know we don't smoke.

Jack   So what were you smoking when I came out?

Anna   Michael'll have some. Come on in, it's getting cold anyhow.

Jack   I do know what marijuana smells like, you know. I wasn't born yesterday. And all I can say is this: I hope to God you never have to prosecute anyone for possessing it. That'd be a bit hypocritical wouldn't it?

Sholto   Come on, let's get you inside.

Jack   I wouldn't mind trying a bit sometime.

Anna   What, dope?

Jack   What's to lose at my age, eh?

Anna   Well, OK, I'll, I mean, I don't think that's a very good idea, Dad –

Jack   You could bake it into a cake. They do that you know. I read it somewhere. And of course it gets into your bloodstream faster that way so you get a better 'high' as they call it.

Anna   OK, Dad, we'll er, certainly think about that . . .

Jack   Good.

He turns round his wheel chair and shoots away. Stops, turns round.

Jack   I was only joking.

Lights down. Music.

Lights up on garden, 9 a.m. next morning. **Jack** *is drinking tea at a garden table. Bees buzz, birds sing, he bats flies away with his newspaper.* **Michael** *is in a deckchair, reading his own newspaper.*

Jack   What do you see when you look at me?

Michael   I'm sorry?

Jack   If you had to describe me to the police, what would you say?

Michael   Why would I be describing you to the police?

Jack   If I'd committed a crime or something.

Michael   Are you thinking of committing a crime?

Jack   No, of course I'm not.

Michael   So why are we having this conversation?

Jack   Old, is what you'd say.

Michael   Sorry?

Jack   He was an old man. That's what you'd say.

Michael   Well, you are old.

Jack   An old man with a stick. Other than that your mind would be blank.

Michael   No it wouldn't.

Jack   Hair colour?

Michael   Grey.

Jack   Skin tone?

Michael   Just, you know –

Jack   Grey.

Michael   I wouldn't say that.

Jack   Size of his nose?

Michael   Average. Normal.

Jack   You see. No idea.

Michael   Can you cut to the chase, Dad?

Jack   Age has become my distinguishing feature. The only one. I'm almost invisible. I could get away with murder.

Michael   That's useful. We could hire you out for contract killings.

Jack   To all intents and purposes, I've ceased to exist. I'm as good as dead.

Michael   What are you talking about, Dad?

Jack   It feels to me like this: the more stories you carry on the inside, the more you fade on the outside. There's some cruel exchange of riches going on.

Michael   You haven't eaten your croissant.

Jack   If you could see all the lamplit rooms inside my head . . . if you could just see –

Michael   You should eat something you know.

Jack   *You* see an old man –

Michael   I don't, I see you, I see my dad –

Jack   – but actually, I'm an Aladdin's cave, I'm a department store at Christmas. I'm a harvest festival. Am I making myself clear?

Michael   OK. D'you want to talk about it?

Jack   Or a ghost train.

Michael   What?

Jack   Have you ever been on a ghost train?

Michael   Years ago.

Jack   They used to terrify the life out of me.

Michael   And why are you bringing them up now?

*He takes **Jack**'s croissant and eats it. Silence.*

Jack   I'm having difficulty sleeping.

Michael   Are you taking your tablets?

Jack   It's not that.

Michael   Maybe you should try hot milk. Or a large brandy.

Jack   I don't know what it is. I'm . . . apprehensive . . .

Michael   Apprehension is the new world order. You get used to it.

Jack   If you got used to it, it wouldn't be apprehension, would it?

Michael   I just mean you learn to live with it in the corners of your mind. Rather than at the forefront.

Jack   It's not in the corners. It's up there in my face. I turn the light out and something catches in my throat, I feel panicky, a taste comes into my mouth like threepenny bits –

Anna comes out. She gives Jack a buff envelope.

Anna   This came. Oh good, you ate all your breakfast. Well done.

She collects up the plates.

Michael   I ate it.

Anna   Oh, for God's sake, he's supposed to get all his nutrients. We're trying to keep your strength up, Dad.

Jack   Why? I'm not entering the Olympics.

Anna   For the wedding. And just because you'll feel better generally.

She continues to clear the table.

Anna   Michael could you get off your arse and give me a hand?

Michael *gets up.*

Jack   I hate to hear a woman say 'arse'.

Anna   Jesus, you can talk, last time we saw the doctor I asked him if he thought you had Tourette's Syndrome.

She stacks up plates.

Jack   You know when I was in hospital?

Anna   Yes?

Jack   I saw my notes. On the bottom, someone had written an 'N' and an 'R'.

Anna   What does that mean?

Jack   I asked a doctor. Not for resuscitation. Whose idea was that?

Anna   What d'you mean? It wasn't anyone's idea.

Jack   Because I know this much: it certainly wasn't mine.

Michael   Are you sure that's what it said?

Jack   I thought you might have told them to do it.

Michael   Who, me?

Jack   No, Anna.

Anna   I didn't ask them to do that. Why would I do such a thing? D'you want me to have a word with the hospital?

Jack   No. It doesn't matter.

Anna   If it doesn't matter why did you bring it up?

Jack   Forget I mentioned it, will you? I'm too tired.

Anna   I'm upset you think it was me, that's all.

Jack   I shouldn't have said that. Sorry.

Anna   Good.

She takes the plates away and goes.

Jack   It was her though.

Michael   It was probably some junior doctor who hadn't been to bed for three days.

Jack I'm not blaming her. She just didn't want me lying there hooked up to a ventilator, pissing into a polythene bag. You'd all quite like me to die really.

Michael Dad –

Jack Not because you hate me, but because I'm becoming a nuisance.

Michael You're not.

Jack Well, not to you maybe, I hardly see you from one year to the next.

Michael Haven't you got any interesting new facts to tell me?

Jack No.

Michael Go on. I bet you have.

Jack I was trying to . . . I was trying . . . earlier . . .

Michael To what?

Jack How old are you again?

Michael Forty-five.

Jack Young.

Michael Not when your wife's left you and you're trying to find a girlfriend and you can't get into any of your trousers anymore. Not when you discover there *is* such a thing as male cellulite. And you've got it. I've even got it on my wrists if I squeeze, look –

He pinches his wrist.

Jack D'you ever get a dark, muffly feeling when you turn the light out at night?

Michael That's the painkillers. Go on, tell me a new fact.

Silence.

Jack D'you know what 'quare' means?

Michael   As in queer? Is this one of your anti-actor jokes?

Jack   It's cartographer's shorthand for 'query'. When they weren't sure of a place name, they'd write 'quare' and fill it in later. But sometimes they forgot. There's a map of Oxfordshire I saw once, that showed a village called Quare, because some dim bloody engraver saw Quare on the original, and thought it must be the name of the place. It appeared on maps for the next hundred years. A mythical village that no-one could ever find.

Michael   Tell me something else.

Jack   Theatrophobia: fear of theatres. Proctophobia: fear of rectums.

Michael   Interesting you should link the two.

Jack   Lutraphobia: fear of otters.

Michael   I think that's enough on the phobic front. What else have you got for me?

Jack   A neutron starts out as a particle, travels as a wave, and arrives as a particle.

Michael   Is that a metaphor or a fact?

Jack   Both.

Michael   Another fact.

Jack   Thanatophobia: fear of death.

Michael   I thought we'd done it with the phobias? Tell me something else.

Jack   My favourite hymn: 'Love Divine, All Love's Excelling'.

Michael   Really?

Jack   Before you were born. Before you were conceived even. I worried there might be something wrong with you. That's a fact.

Michael   What d'you mean 'wrong'?

Jack   I can't remember now. I worried about having children who were . . . blighted in some way.

Michael   Well luckily we're both perfect.

Pause.

Jack   I saw a flower in the garden yesterday. Purple, almost black, with a yellow centre, like a dark, velvety primrose. As soon as I saw it, I started to cry and I don't know why. I think I picked one for my mother once. I can remember the soft snap of the stem. From seventy years ago.

Michael   How old were you when she died?

Jack   Six. I still dream about her. I'm getting this a lot just now. A particular memory, something tiny, will floor me, stop me in my tracks. Not big things. A door handle. A scent. A piece of fabric. I don't know what all this stuff means. I don't know why it knocks me sideways.

Michael *is awkward with the potential for emotional disclosure. He clears his throat.*

Michael   Well, maybe it's, I mean, you know, the tablets have a bit of an effect, maybe they're making you feel a bit –

He look at his watch.

Did you take your last lot by the way? Anna!

Jack   Tragedy. The song of a lonely billy goat.

Michael   What?

Jack   You wanted facts. Tragedy. That's what it means. From the Greek. The cry of the billy goat. Separated from the females, abandoned on an island, and bleating his lonely song.

Michael   Is that how you see yourself? As a tragic billy goat?

Jack   I've got an electric wheelchair. I have a fridge, a
microwave. The famous deep fat fryer. Central heating. A
television. A video if I could work out how to use it. Hot
water any time I want it. Turn on the tap and there it is. I
have two good suits and my socks are pure wool. Assorted
shirts and pants. Good strong brogues. Soft shoes for sore
feet. Espadrilles, a present from Anna, never worn because
they make me feel as if I'm tipping over backwards. I have a
wedding ring. My own teeth. I have many books and some
rare maps. A flush toilet. A bath and a shower. A small
Persian rug and three pairs of spectacles to cover all
eventualities. Have I left anything out?

Michael   Two children.

Jack   No-one, so far, has burst into my home in the night
and tried to kill me. I've never been arrested at three a.m.
by men in balaclavas and imprisoned without trial. I'm not
expecting this to happen. There are some mercies.

Michael   It's not been a bad life then.

Jack   How do you know?

Michael   Well hasn't it?

Jack   There are all sorts of things you don't know about
me.

Michael   There are all sorts of things you don't know
about me.

Jack   Such as?

Michael   You first.

Pause.

Jack   D'you think you take after me?

Michael   I hope not.

Jack   Why?

Michael   Because you're a crabbed, bad-tempered, stubborn –

Jack   Cunt.

Michael   You said it.

Jack   You don't know with children. You don't know what you're getting. Mostly me, mostly your mother, or someone else completely. . . I worried about it . . . Are you glad I made you go to Church?

Michael   No.

Jack   I thought you might have appreciated the certainties. I always did.

Michael   You're obsessed with certainties.

Jack   What else is there? I sent you to Church to give you a structure.

Michael   I hated it. I hated the cold and the smell and the gloom, I hated the po-faced sanctity. I hated the way it made me feel like a bad person. The only bit I liked was the vestments. Purple for funerals and Good Friday. White for Christmas and Easter Sunday. Green for run of the mill Sundays when it wasn't a sung mass and everyone had colds and snorted and coughed and there was never any heating. All that fucking money, the Vatican looks like a Liberace love fest and we all got chilblains listening to some dodgy pederast urging us to bang our chests and cry mea culpa.

Jack   Was the priest a pederast? I never knew that.

Michael   All priests were pederasts in those days. Don't you read the papers, Dad?

Anna *comes out.*

Anna   Were you calling me?

Michael   Was I? Oh yeah, I think he needs his tablets.

Jack   I've just had them.

Anna He's just had them.

Michael When?

Jack Before breakfast, Jesus, what d'you take me for?

Michael Sorry. I didn't realise you'd had them. Sorry.

Anna Dad, can I just say that it wasn't me who told them you weren't for resuscitation.

Jack Who was it then?

Anna I don't know. It was a mistake.

Jack Where's Sholto's mother? What'shername.

Anna Portia. She's called Portia.

Jack All right, all right.

Anna Did you like her?

Jack She's all right.

Anna Meaning?

Jack I'm not sure we've got much in common.

Anna How d'you know, you've only just met her?

Jack Look, if you like her, that's all that matters. She's not going to be *my* mother-in-law is she?

Anna Just try and make an effort, Dad, will you? Make her feel welcome.

Jack What d'you mean? What d'you want me to do?

Anna Don't grunt and don't swear, she's a Christian.

Jack So am I.

Michael She's the non-swearing, non-offensive variety.

Jack All right, all right.

Portia, **Sholto**'s *mother, comes out with* **Sholto**. *She's West Indian, sixty-ish.*

Portia   I've just seen her wedding dress. She's going to look gorgeous.

Jack   And you're looking ravishing yourself, Portia.

Michael   We said be nice, Dad, we didn't say chat her up.

Portia   Thank you, Jack, that's very kind of you. You're not looking so bad either.

Sholto   I've just been showing Mum your maps, Jack.

Jack   I hope you were careful with them.

Anna   Of course he was –

Sholto's *mobile rings.*

Sholto   Excuse me –

He answers it.

Hello?

Sholto *listens.*

Portia   His work never goes away. Middle of the night he's taking calls.

Sholto   Damn, damn, damn, bugger . . . shit . . . OK, OK, we'll sort it out, don't worry –

Jack   Who's he representing this time?

Portia   One of the dancers he's using for the wedding.

Anna   They were going to give him exceptional leave to remain but it doesn't sound good –

Sholto   Don't worry, give me your number, hang on – (*To* **Jack** *and* **Portia**.) excuse me a minute will you –

Sholto *goes out.*

Jack   Why are we giving bloody dancers political asylum?

Michael   Why not?

Anna   Actually, Dad, he's a tailor. Who happens to be able to dance.

Jack   He's taking the piss.

Anna   You don't know anything about it, Dad. He was tortured.

Jack *is uncomfortable.*

Jack   So he says.

Michael   Just stop, will you –

Sholto *comes back.*

Anna   Is everything OK?

Sholto   Yeah, yeah, he's just panicking. They haven't turned him down yet, he misunderstood a letter.

Jack   So what did you make of them then?

Portia   I'm sorry?

Jack   My maps.

Portia   Oh. Very beautiful. The one with the dancing girls and camels and all those strange beasts –

Jack   Everyone goes on about that one. You'd think it was the only one he'd ever made. And it's not even a proper map. It's just a bit of old nonsense.

Portia   It's Arabia, isn't it? And the bottom bit would be what's now the Yemen.

Jack (*sharply*)   How d'you know that?

Portia   I used to teach geography.

Jack   Oh. Well, anyway, he never actually went there, as far as we know . . .

Portia   Obviously, or he wouldn't have filled it with mermaids and three-headed bulls.

Jack   The West Indies, America maybe, we know he went there, but not Arabia.

Anna   D'you think this Dido woman came from the West Indies? The one he married?

Jack   Oh don't start this again –

Michael   I thought it was a fling, not a marriage?

Anna   No, I think he married her.

Jack   Who?

Anna   Our ancestor, Thomas Goode, had a black servant called Dido.

Michael   You don't actually know that. There was someone called Dido and there was a black servant, you don't know they were the same woman.

Anna   It has to be.

Portia   And?

Anna   So we're quite possibly descended from a black woman. Don't you think it's brilliant?

Sholto   What's brilliant about it?

Anna   It just means, it means, you know –

Michael   We too can have our own claim to victimhood.

Anna   It means we have a deeper connection, Sholto and me –

Michael   Does it bollocks –

Anna   It does –

Sholto   It doesn't. We already have a connection. It's got nothing to do with who your great great great great grandmother was –

Anna   But if she was black –

Jack   Well, I'm not convinced –

Portia   And you're not black, darling, anymore than Sholto's white. Black's the colour of your skin, not your blood. Black's not a hidden thing. Black's out there and in your face.

Sholto   You're white, honey.

Anna   Christ, I'm not saying I'm not –

Michael   Good, because that would be absurd –

Sholto   What is it you're trying to say?

Michael   So some ancestor was black – possibly – and consequently we should feel what? Better? More interesting? A little bit black?

Anna   I just think it's interesting that's all. I never said anything about being a bit black. Thomas Goode's first wife had a black female servant who was very tall and beautiful apparently, and hugely admired by everyone who met her –

Michael   Now we're getting down to it. If she'd had wall to wall hips and a squint, it wouldn't have crossed your mind to claim her as your own.

Anna   In the records, if you look closely, it says he married 'Dido Smith, a servant of this parish' in seventeen ninety-three, in a secret ceremony, presumably to legitimise the only child he had. Our ancestor, Georgiana Goode.

Jack   I'm lost.

Michael   But was the black servant called Dido ?

Anna   Well it doesn't actually say, but they always gave black servants classical names, no matter what they were called originally. Pompey, Cato, that sort of thing.

Portia   And where did she come from, this Dido?

Anna   Nobody seems to know where she came from originally. We know he owned plantations –

Michael   – but the slave owning bit's not something we like to shout about.

Anna   – so he probably brought her over from the West Indies.

Sholto   It's supposition, not documentary fact though –

Anna   I'm saying it's a possibility, that's all. All I'm saying is that we might be descended from a slave owner, but we're also descended from a slave.

Michael   Oh phew, and one cancels out the other? What a relief.

Sholto   OK, so maybe you're right. But what does it mean now? And does it actually matter?

Anna   It just means we're more interconnected than we like to think.

Sholto   It doesn't matter where you came from in the past. All that matters is how you behave now, and how you're treated now.

Anna   Well I'm sorry, but I've felt . . . tainted . . . you know I have Sholto, you know I've felt uncomfortable knowing I'm descended from a slave owner. And yes OK, this makes me feel better. I'm sorry, but it does take away some of the moral opprobrium I feel I've been carrying –

Sholto   Not on my behalf. Have I ever passed judgement, have I ever said anything at all except that you're not responsible for something that happened two hundred years ago? You might have had an ancestor who was an incestuous child molester –

Portia   Sholto!

Sholto   – or burnt witches, but it would be odd, not to say irrational, if you were losing sleep over it now –

Anna   I just happen to feel a little guilty, that's all I'm saying.

Sholto   But guilt is the most useless emotion, it's corrosive and inward looking and it gets you nowhere –

Anna   God I wish I'd never brought this up, it's a small thing I thought was interesting, that's all. I'm sorry I mentioned it. Excuse me.

She storms out. Pause.

Jack   She's very touchy at the moment.

Lights down.

Music.

Lights up on garden later: The sun is going down, **Anna**, **Sholto** *and* **Michael** *are lighting lanterns and candles, setting a garden table for supper.* **Jack** *is sitting in a chair with his eyes closed, a buff envelope on his lap, and* **Portia**, *sits next to him, reading a newspaper aloud to him.*

Portia (*reading*)   'Woman's torso found in the Thames' . . . Why do they want to go chopping women up like that? People are very sick . . . 'Three hundred and sixty illegal immigrants found in a ship's hold at Portsmouth yesterday, seventy-six of whom had died of thirst and/or suffocation . . .' Now that is a terrible thing, Jack.

Jack *stirs.*

Jack   What?

Portia   To suffocate and die like that. Just when you think your trials are coming to an end.

Jack (*confused*)   What?

Portia   I've been reading the paper to you.

Jack   Didn't hear a thing.

Portia   That's just as well because it's all very depressing. Everyone raping and killing and starving to death. Shouting and scandalising and accusing each other. You don't want to hear these things, they'll make you despair.

Jack I've given up reading the papers. I don't want to know about the world anymore. Everything seems to come round again in a different hat.

She puts the paper down.

Portia Anyway. This is a lovely place you have here, Jack.

Jack Nothing to do with me. It's Anna's. I'm just the old man in the attic.

Portia Anna has made my Sholto very happy, d'you know that?

Jack Sholto. What sort of name's that then?

Portia We named him after the doctor who delivered him. He treated us so well, such a kind man, and it was very welcome let me tell you, in those days, to be shown this sort of respect. The very first week my husband and I got here, we went to Church, and you know the vicar shook our hands afterwards and said, 'Thank you so much for coming, but I'd be grateful if you didn't come back. My congregation aren't comfortable with black people.'

Jack He probably meant well.

Portia In what possible way could he have meant well?

Jack Yes, well, things were different then. You can't judge the past by the present.

Portia When we first came here, I said to my husband, look at all these factories, nothing but factories everywhere. Because you know this was the fifties, and there was smoke coming from all the chimneys in rows and rows of terraced houses, and I thought they must be factories, they were so long, so endless. They didn't look like houses at all. Joe said to me, these are homes Portia, this is where they live, and I was shocked. They're all the same, I said, how do they know which one belongs to them? I didn't l know about house numbers you see.

Jack D'you not have house numbers in Barbados?

Portia   Barbuda.

Jack   I thought that was a type of fish.

Portia   You're thinking of barracuda.

Jack   Can you eat it?

Portia   Yes.

Jack   What does it taste like?

Portia   Fish.

Jack   I like a nice chop.

Portia   Have you ever been to the Caribbean, Jack?

Jack   I'm not very good with heat.

Portia   Barbuda's very beautiful.

Jack   Or insects. I like a temperate climate.

Portia   The rain can be a bit depressing though, don't you think?

Jack   I don't mind rain.

Anna   Dad doesn't like travelling.

Jack   No. What's wrong with that?

Anna   He doesn't even like London.

Jack   I like the North. I don't want to go anywhere else. If I want to know about another country I'll look at a map. What would I learn about Spain by sitting in a hotel full of people from Birmingham? Absolutely nothing, that's what. A map tells you all you need to know.

Portia   My uncle in Barbuda had all of the Ordnance survey maps of England. Before I came over I spent weeks poring over them. I thought it would help me know my way around, get a feel of the place. I was only sixteen, I didn't realise. They were no use at all to me in the middle of London.

Jack *picks up the envelope from his lap.*

Jack   I've got an update on the family tree here, if anyone fancies a look.

Michael   God, Dad, do we have to?

Portia   I'll take a look at them Jack.

Anna   Michael I think it's time . . . ?

She nods at **Michael** *who goes out.* **Jack** *takes papers from the envelope. Lays them out on the table.*

Jack   See? Right back to the seventeenth century, with a few gaps. English through and through.

Anna *comes over and looks at the papers.*

Anna   There's a Maddock in there. The Maddocks were Welsh.

Jack   They're not, they're from Cheshire. That's what it says here.

Anna   Yes, but originally they're from Wales.

Jack   Our lot aren't. It doesn't say anything about being Welsh anywhere.

Sholto   Maddock's probably a Breton name originally.

Jack   Yes, well *originally*, I mean originally –

Portia   We all came from Africa. Mitochondrial Eve.

Jack   Look, we're an English family –

Anna   And the Armstrongs were Border Reivers, they were back and forwards to Scotland all the time

Jack   There might be a drop of Welsh or Scots –

Sholto   And Rogan 's Irish.

Jack   And all right, a bit of Irish –

Jack *traces the outline of the map sensuously.*

Jack   Look at these names . . . '*Florence Edna Maddock . . .
Amelia Eveline Cartwright . . . Josiah Archimedes Armstrong, glove-
maker . . . Georgiana Persephone Goode, Benjamin Thomas Goode,
clerk*' . . . We came from these people. All our genes and
whatnot. If we saw their portraits, we'd find ourselves there.

Portia   We go back to William the Conqueror, don't we
Sholto?

Sholto   On one side.

Jack   I thought William the Conqueror was French.

Portia   Someone from the university showed us. A
genealogical historian.

Jack   He's having you on.

Sholto   She.

Jack   How does she figure that out then?

Sholto   D'you know anything about Barbuda?

Portia   He thinks it's a type of fish.

Sholto   Well it's very small, and most of the slave families
who were taken there came from the same villages in West
Africa. And they were kept together, not broken up like
most families, because the guy who owned the island was
slightly more enlightened than most. He came from
Leicestershire, and all the people he sent out to Barbuda as
blacksmiths, carpenters and whatever, were local people
from his estates. People whose families had come over with
the Conqueror hundreds of years before and stayed with
their feudal overlord. And of course they intermarried in
Barbuda, and here we are today. Direct descendants of
people who came over with William the First. All of which is
interesting, but of no earthly use to anyone. If someone's
intent on kicking your head in, how much good is it going to
do you to tell them you're a direct descendant of William
the Conqueror. 'Oh I beg your pardon sir, I thought you
were black –'

Michael (*off*) Sholto? Can you come and give me a hand?

Sholto   Coming.

Sholto goes out.

Jack   A hand with what?

*Sholto comes back with **Michael**, carrying a huge roll of stiff paper, seven or eight feet long.*

Sholto   Da-dah!

Anna   Before we eat, Dad –

Jack   What the hell's that?

Sholto   A present –

Jack   What sort of present?

Michael   For you –

Anna   And you'd better like it, Dad, because it was a pig to get made, and cost us the price of a small house –

*Anna, **Michael** and **Sholto** unroll the paper onto the ground, holding down the corners with chairs. Simultaneously, the photograph, for that is what it is, is projected onto the back wall: it's an aerial photo of a city with some streets and houses shaded in red. It's strangely beautiful. The red forms a sort of shimmering grid.*

Jack   What is it?

Michael   It was my idea. It's a map of your life.

Jack   What?

Anna kneels down and points at one of the places in red.

Anna   Look, this is where you were born. Near the river, look.

*On the projection, we see the place to which she refers light up slightly. **Jack** stares at it, bewildered.*

Jack   Why've you bought me this?

Anna   It's just a present.

Jack   It's not my birthday is it?

Michael   We thought you'd like it, that's all –

Jack   It's not my birthday until December.

Michael   And then you moved to this house here – look, Dad –

Again it lights up on the projection.

Anna   With Auntie Ginny.

Portia   It's beautiful Jack.

Sholto   So you travelled from here . . .

He traces the outline of streets shaded in red. The projection light follows his tracing.

. . . to here.

Anna   And this is where you went to school –

It lights up on the projection. (This happens with every place they point out.)

Michael   It's not actually there anymore, there's a Tesco's there now –

Sholto   And this is where you had your first job, on Pilgrim Street –

Michael   And then you move along here, down here, and here's St. Cuthbert's where you got married . . .

Anna   And then this is where you had us, this house here, see it?

Michael   And then we moved here.

The grid of streets glow on the projection.

Sholto   And now you're here.

He points to a house a distance away from the others. It glows on the projection.

Anna   This is where you are now.

Jack *stares at the map in silence.*

Sholto   What d'you think?

Jack   I don't . . . it's . . . I don't know what to say.

Anna   D'you like it?

Jack   It's . . . I thought it . . . Is that it?

Anna   What d'you mean?

Jack   I thought it would look like more than that.

Anna   What d'you mean?

Jack   It's just some coloured marks on a page. I thought it'd be more complicated than that. I thought my life would look like more than that.

Anna   It's just a map.

Jack   Didn't make much of a mark did I?

Michael   Oh, I don't know.

Pause.

Anna   So . . . d'you like it?

Jack *holds out an arm to* **Sholto**.

Sholto   You want to get up?

Jack   Down.

Anna   What?

Sholto *helps him to his feet.*

Sholto   What is it you want to do?

Jack   I want to touch it.

Sholto   Oh, right, OK . . . Can you manage?

They help him to his knees.

Michael   Is that OK?

Jack   Thank you.

He traces the outlines of the red streets with his fingers. He starts to cry. A tear falls onto the photo. On the projection, we see a blot fall onto the grid of red streets.

Fade down lights.

Act Two.

Lights, music up. Garden. Evening. The map still glows at the back.
Sholto *is watching the dancers rehearsing with the band. The dance*
comes to an end. **Sholto** *claps.*

Sholto   Thank you. It's going to be great, guys. Well
done. I'll see you down the pub in fifteen minutes, I've just
got a couple of calls to make.

As the dancers and band go out **Anna** *appears from the shadows with
a glass of wine.*

Sholto   Were you watching that?

Anna   Some of it.

Sholto   You're not supposed to see it till it's ready. It's not
ready yet.

Anna   Oh well. Too late.

Sholto   So what d'you think? I think it's fantastic, but they
keep telling me it needs a bit of fine tuning.

Anna   It's fine.

Sholto   Is that it?

Anna   What d'you mean?

Sholto   Just a non-committal 'fine'?

Anna   It's great.

Sholto   It's going to be bloody brilliant actually.

Anna   All right, it's brilliant.

Sholto   What's the matter with you?

Anna   Nothing.

Sholto   Don't you want them to dance at the wedding?

Anna   Yes.

Sholto   So could you be a bit more enthusiastic, d'you think? I've got all these guys together, they've pooled all their knowledge, all the stuff that separates them and they've managed to invent something new –

Anna   Jesus, Sholto, I do realise that –

Sholto   They've put their heart and soul into this thing, and all you can muster is 'great.' Some of them are under threat of deportation, and instead of tearing their hair out they're working out choreography for our wedding –

Anna   OK, I'm sorry. I'm sorry.

Sholto   What's the matter with you?

Anna   You just asked me that. Nothing.

Sholto   You're being very weird.

Anna   *I'm* being weird?

Sholto   And now you're doing this thing where you talk in secret code –

Anna   What d'you mean, secret code –

Sholto   Where I'm supposed to interpret what you mean from a series of cryptic remarks, and whatever I say, you hand it back to me inside out.

Anna   I said you were being weird –

Sholto   Actually, you didn't say that, *I* said it. You implied it, but you didn't say it –

Anna   All right, I'm saying it now, straight up, how un-cryptic is this: you're being very fucking weird.

Sholto   Why? What have I done?

Anna   And now you're pretending you don't know. God I hate it when you do this –

Sholto   When I do what? What am I supposed to have done?

Anna   Well, you humiliated me in front of my family and your mother for a start.

Sholto   When?

Anna   All I did was mention that an ancestor of mine happens to have been black and you all jump on me.

Sholto   Oh, for God's sake –

Anna   I mean Michael I can understand, he'll argue about anything, but there was no need for you to agree with him –

Sholto   But I do agree with him.

Anna   That's not the point!

Sholto   So what is the point?

Anna   The point is you don't take Michael's side because you're not marrying Michael, you're marrying me. You made me look a complete arse in front of everyone, and then even your mother joined in, as if I was suggesting I'm black or something, which God knows isn't what I meant at all and you know it –

Sholto   She wasn't joining in, she was just saying she likes you the way you are, you don't have to acquire an African ancestor to gain her acceptance –

Anna   That's not what I was doing –

Sholto   So what were you doing?

Anna   You're doing it again!

Sholto   What? What the hell am I doing?

Anna   You're deliberately misconstruing everything I say! I didn't do anything to 'gain acceptance', I just made an interesting discovery and foolishly thought other people might find it as interesting as I did, but obviously not, obviously everyone else has some agenda of their own which they feel obliged to offload onto me –

Sholto   Anna you're overreacting –

Anna   I'm forty years old, I've never been married before and I'm frightened, why can't you see that?

Sholto *is momentarily floored.*

Sholto   Because hey, hold on a minute, excuse me . . . this is a completely new tack, I'm not a bloody mind reader, we're not talking about you being frightened of getting married –

Anna   I am, that's exactly what I've been saying –

Sholto   When?

Anna   Just now –

Sholto   Well you've been doing it in code then, and it completely slipped my notice.

Anna   What are you talking about?

Sholto   What am *I* talking about? Jesus, you need a depth charger to work out your subtexts –

Anna   What 'subtexts'?

Sholto   Anna, stop!

Anna   Three of my friends got divorced last year. Three!

Sholto   Is that what this is about?

Anna   I don't see the point of getting married if you're only going to get divorced. I mean why do it?

Sholto   We're not going to get divorced.

Anna   How do we know that?

Sholto   OK, we don't –

Anna   You see!

Sholto   I'm never going to leave you, how's that?

Anna   Oh this is stupid, we're getting married and it's too late to do anything about it now.

Sholto   D'you want to do something about it?

Anna   I was just expressing anxiety, that's all, am I not allowed to express anxiety now?

Sholto   OK, anxiety expressed, crisis over. Come to the pub.

Anna   Sholto, just tell me that it is actually interesting about my ancestor. And then I'll shut up, I promise.

Sholto   How interesting is it that one of my lot came over with William the Conqueror?

Anna   Very.

Sholto   But that's all any of it is: very interesting, and so what?

Anna *is awkward.*

Anna   I'm pregnant –

Sholto *hardly has time look delighted before* **Jack**'s *voice shatters the moment.*

Jack   Somebody?

Jack *comes out in his pyjamas, leaning on a walking stick. He looks frail. He wanders around the garden, disorientated.*

Anna   Dad, what are you doing?

Jack   There was music out here. It woke me up.

Sholto   Sorry Jack, that was me –

Anna   Come back to bed, come on.

She takes his arm.

Jack   I need to sit a while.

He sits down.

Jack   Listen.

Silence.

Anna   What?

Jack   There are some birds still up. Listen.

They listen.

Jack   There's a gibbous moon.

Anna   Yes, there is.

Jack   I've seen nine hundred and twelve full moons.

Pause.

Doesn't seem that many.

Pause.

Jack   Nine hundred and twelve times I've looked up and seen a round white disc in the night sky. The moon's more comforting than the sun, don't you think?

Anna   I suppose it is.

Jack   I wonder how many more I'll see.

Sholto   Lots. Loads and loads.

Jack   After I go it'll still be there. Waxing and waning, month after month, year after year.

Pause.

Jack   Bloody relentless isn't it?

Anna   Let's get you back inside.

Jack   From my bed to the bathroom's twenty-three steps. But it's only nineteen on the way back. What's that about?

Anna   I can't think.

Jack   I can only assume the difference has something to do with the relative fullness of my bladder.

Anna   Give me your arm.

Jack   I've got more of a spring in my step on the way back. Less of a shuffle.

Anna   Why are you counting your steps to the lavatory?

Jack   Just keeping an eye on things.

Anna   It seems a terrible waste of energy.

Jack   I've seen seventy-six Christmases.

Anna   Come on, let's go inside.

Jack   Eaten eighty-two thousand, nine hundred and ninety-two meals.

Anna   If you're going to sit out here, would you like Sholto to get you a rug?

Jack   Give or take the odd occasion when I've missed a meal or two, but snacks probably make up for the short fall. A hundred and fifty-two thousand, eight hundred and eighty cups of tea.

Sholto   D'you want me to get a rug?

Jack   I've woken up on twenty-seven thousand, nine hundred and forty consecutive mornings, discounting a few sick days when I slept through till the afternoon. Married one wife, fathered two children. Who are now adult strangers. And that's it. Finished.

Sholto   It's not finished, Jack.

Jack *looks away.*

Jack   I thought it might have amounted to more than that.

Anna   You can't measure your life out in cups of tea and the number of meals you've eaten.

Jack   How are you going to measure yours?

Anna   I don't know, why would I want to measure it anyway?

Jack   You could count all the things you've ever owned. One BMW, two Saabs and a lot of kitchen appliances.

Anna   Dad –

Jack   A few hundred people successfully prosecuted and sent to jail. At least you've kept crime off the streets. That'll be a satisfying reassurance for you as they turn off your life support machine.

Anna   Actually, Dad, I don't think my life's been a waste of time.

Jack   Don't you?

Anna   No. And I don't prosecute anymore. I defend. It's not trivial, it's not a waste of anyone's time, it's vital, unless you fancy living in a police state. I don't see it as a waste at all. Why would I?

Jack   Because generally speaking, it is. It's just shouting into the wind. And then it's over.

Sholto   Is that what you think, Jack?

Jack   I used to think death was a person. You know, with a hood and a sickle. There's something comforting in it, at least it's corporeal, it's *some*thing as opposed to *no*thing. It's the nothing that turns my bowels to water.

Silence.

Jack   You can take me back to bed now.

Sholto *goes to him. Blackout. Music.*

Lights up on garden, early evening. **Anna**, **Sholto**, **Michael**, **Portia** *and* **Jack** *are playing cards and drinking wine.* **Michael** *is drinking Scotch and tipsy.*

Michael   OK. Antes in.

Jack   What?

Anna   Ten pence, Dad. The ante's ten pence.

Jack   What do I do with it?

Sholto   Put it in the middle – here –

He takes **Jack**'s *money and puts it in the middle of the table. They all* *look at their cards and rearrange them in silence.*

Jack   Now what?

Michael   It's poker, Dad, you're supposed to keep stum.

Anna   I'll play with Dad, all right?

Michael   You can't play two hands, you can either play his hand or your own, you can't play two –

Anna   All right, all right, it's only a game, Michael –

Portia   What are we playing again?

Sholto   For God's sake, Mum, poker.

Portia   I know that but I've got seven cards here.

Michael   It's seven card stud.

Jack   I thought it was poker?

Anna   That is poker, Dad –

Portia   I'm used to five card stud –

Michael   Anna if you're going to play with Dad we'll have to start again –

He collects in the cards and shuffles the pack.

Portia   Oh damn, I had a straight flush too.

Michael   OK, re-dealing –

He re-deals as **Sholto***'s phone goes.*

Sholto   Hello?

Jack   I wish someone would tell me the rules.

Sholto   OK, I'll sort that out first thing in the morning . . .

Jack   What are we playing this time?

Michael   Poker. Five card stud. Threes are wild.

Jack   I've no idea what's going on.

Anna   I'll help, let's see your cards.

Sholto   Leave it with me. I'll make sure all the documentation's in place. Don't worry. OK.

He turns off the phone and looks at his cards.

Sholto   Sorry everyone.

Portia   The trick is to keep a poker face, Jack.

Michael   It's an acting job, Dad. You mustn't give anything away.

Jack *looks at the cards in* **Anna***'s hand.*

Jack   There's a three there –

Michael   Shut up, Dad, will you?

Jack   Shut up yourself. What did you say a three meant?

Anna   It's a wild card, it can be anything you want it to be.

Jack   I'm lost.

Michael   Oh, for God's sake!

Jack   Well I don't know how to play bloody poker. Why can't we play pontoon?

Michael   Because poker's a better game, that's why.

Jack   Not if you don't know how to play, it's not.

Portia   We can play pontoon, Jack, I don't mind. How does it go?

Jack   I can't remember.

Michael   Why don't we play poker and you can watch?

He pours himself another large whisky.

Jack   What did you say about an acting job?

Sholto   It's just you're not supposed to let on what you've got in your hand. You have to bluff. So if you've got a bad hand you have to act as if you've got a brilliant hand.

Jack   Acting. He loves that.

Michael   Will you stop talking about me as if I'm not here?

Portia   D'you get to see Michael on the stage much, Jack?

Jack   Never.

Sholto   He's very good you know.

Michael   Thank you.

Jack   I wouldn't know, I've never seen him.

Portia   You've never seen your own son on stage? Shame on you, Jack.

Jack   I'm not a theatre sort of person.

Sholto   What does that mean?

Michael   Are we playing poker or what?

Anna   Well you know I've got a three so I think you'd better deal again –

Michael   Oh, for fuck's sake –

He gathers in the cards again.

And you're not playing, Dad, right?

Jack   I saw a pantomime once. This is when I was lad. There was a woman in tights pretending to be a man. Bloody awful.

Sholto   You should see Michael, you know. I think he'd like you to.

Michael   Honestly Sholto, there's no point having this conversation. He's frightened to go to the theatre in case it makes him a homosexual. OK, who's playing?

Jack   Anyway, it's too late now. Can't hold my bladder for long enough. If people tell me he's good, I'm prepared to believe them.

Michael   Well that's a major concession –

Jack   But I don't have to sit through it to find out. Why can't people have proper jobs anymore? What's wrong with knuckling down? I was a bookkeeper for forty odd years and I hated every minute of it –

Michael   Well more fool you then –

Jack   It put food on the table, it supported a family –

Michael *knocks back his whisky and pours himself another.*

Michael   Oh well, cheers, Dad. Cheers everyone. Might as well live up to an actor's reputation for being fond of a drop. Don't want to let the side down do we?

Jack   Go on, make an arse of yourself –

Michael   Just give me a couple of these and soon I'll be calling you darling and shagging your dog. I'll be checking into rehab and dyeing my hair. I'll talk too loudly, I'll be completely self absorbed, and I'll bore for England about what I said to Paul Scofield in a green room in nineteen fifty-three. You can all call me a luvvie and will I find that insulting, patronising and philistine? Of course I won't, because it's just the English way isn't it –

Jack   All right, all right, we get the joke –

Michael   Oh, but we love a joke, don't we? Don't want anyone getting too big for their boots, so we'll take the piss, it's just a bit of fun, but let's face it, actors are all arseholes aren't they, I know they are, I've seen them on the TV banging on about themselves, you can't take them seriously. Unless of course they're American, but you see they're stars, which is a different thing altogether. Your English luvvie, on the other hand, deserves all he gets, including the multi – purpose contempt of fat fuckers who sit on their arses all day thinking I could do that, even though the only cue they've ever picked up is on a snooker table. I mean we're basically just show-offs, aren't we, Dad? It's not art, it's just ego, I'm in danger of drawing too much attention to myself, and we can't have that, can we, Dad? You know what I think? I think we're just a receptacle for all the prejudices you can't find a home for anymore. You've got to hate someone and you can't hate cripples or Muslims or blacks anymore but fuck me, there's always actors –

Anna   Michael –

Michael   – only let's call them luvvies in a kind of world weary contemptuous way which belies the fact you're some miserable fucking bookkeeper, or a midget accountant in grey shoes with the imaginative life of a mollusc who thinks he's being *witty* for Christ's sake, oh, you're in on the joke about actors, you've read *Private Eye,* you found a copy on a bus once, God, you make me puke –

Anna   Michael –

Michael   I'm never going to be a lawyer or a brain surgeon, Dad. Get over it.

Pause. He sways.

Excuse me. I'm a bit drunk.

He picks up the bottle and goes out. Silence.

Jack   Shall we play pontoon then?

Blackout.

Lights up on garden, morning.
Jack *is sitting dozing in a chair.* **Portia** *comes out with a tray of tea.*

Portia   I brought you some tea.

Jack (*stirring*)   What?

Portia   Tea.

Jack   Oh. Thank you.

She sets it down and pours. Sits down next to him.

Portia   How you feeling this morning?

Jack   Fine, thank you.

They sip. Awkward hiatus.

Jack   Sorry about my son.

Portia   Sorry?

Jack   My son. Last night.

Portia   Everyone gets a bit over-excited preparing for a wedding.

Jack   I suppose so.

Silence.

Jack   So did you want something then?

Portia   What d'you mean, did I want something?

Jack   Have you not got things to do?

Portia   Such as what?

Jack   I don't know. Wedding things. Hats and what not.

Portia   That's all taken care of. Your daughter's a great organiser

Jack   A wedding used to be a walk down the aisle, a couple of hymns, then a hotel on the sea front for a ham salad and a glass of Asti Spumante.

Portia   I could never abide an English salad. There was terrible stuff in tins, you don't get it any more, bits of peas and carrots in salad cream. Tinned sick, Sholto used to call it.

Jack   Then there was a slice of wedding cake and the bride and groom buggered off to Scarborough for the weekend. And that was that till one or other of them dropped dead.

They drink their tea in silence.

Jack   Do you and Sholto talk much?

Portia   No. His sister is the talker but she's in Australia now.

Jack   I mean talk properly.

Portia   I know you do. And no, he doesn't.

Jack   No. They don't.

Silence.

Portia   Is there something particular you wanted to talk to them about?

Jack   Not really. I don't know.

Silence.

Jack   My lot have a special loud voice they use when they talk to me. Do yours do that?

Portia   No. Mine edit. They think I don't know about certain things. Sex mostly. They think they're protecting me, you know?

Jack   There was a man, when I was a boy, used to stand in the woods with his pants down and his whatsit out. And we never told a soul, because we thought our parents would be shocked. We thought they didn't know about these sort of things. We were protecting them from sex, even though we didn't know it *was* sex. It was just poor Charlie Patterson with his thing out, because he had shell-shock and lived with his mother.

Portia   When I first started teaching none of the children knew anything about sex. Now they're discussing the merits of flavoured condoms at seven.

Jack   I never got any qualifications. I'm what you call an autodidact.

Portia   If you could have done anything, what would you have liked to have done?

Jack   I'm sorry?

Portia   What sort of job?

Pause.

Jack   I always fancied being an opera singer.

Portia   You sing then?

Jack   No, not really.

Portia   So why an opera singer?

Jack   I like the music. You get to hold people's attention, give them goose pimples, cry, laugh, whatever. And then you get applause. All those people appreciating what you've done. There's not much applause in bookkeeping.

A beat.

Portia   Has it crossed your mind that might be where Michael gets his acting from?

Jack   No, that's different. I'm talking about singing here. Different kettle of fish entirely.

Portia   I see.

Pause.

Sholto wanted to be a dancer when he was young. We persuaded him against it. We wanted him to have a profession. I always wonder if we did the right thing.

Jack   Too late now.

Portia   Yes.

Silence.

Jack   Anyway. I'm sure you've got better things to do than sit here talking to me.

Portia   I've already told you I haven't.

Pause.

Portia   Anna told me your house burnt down. That must have been terrible.

Jack   I didn't do it deliberately.

Portia   Of course not.

Jack   Chip pan.

Portia   And were you there at the time?

Jack   I was out.

Portia   And you managed to save all your maps and everything? That was a lucky thing Jack.

Jack   Yes, well I happened to have them to hand.

She pours tea.

Portia   Was it a nice house?

Jack   It was all right.

Pause.

Jack   It had an empty feel. I don't mind being on my own. But I like to know someone's there.

Portia   And now you're with Anna and Sholto. So it worked out in the end.

Jack   I didn't do it deliberately.

Portia   I never said that.

Jack *shifts uneasily.*

Jack   I can't remember if I took my tablets or not –

Portia   You took three at breakfast time, I saw you.

Jack   Did I?

Portia   You did.

Silence.

Jack   Looks like the weather's going to hold then.

Portia   It does.

Jack   You don't want to get married in the rain if you can help it.

Portia   Did you have good weather for your wedding?

Jack   Pissed down.

Portia   Oh dear.

Jack   We didn't care.

Portia   What was your wife's name?

Jack   Rose. And here's a funny thing: it was my mother's name too.

Pause.

Both dead now. All the roses are dead.

Silence.

Jack   I've been saving up my sleeping tablets.

Portia   You have?

Jack   Don't tell the children.

Portia   I wouldn't dream of doing such a thing.

Jack   I don't think I'm going to get better, you see. I don't want the children to know.

Portia   I won't say a word.

Jack   I get a terrible feeling at night when I turn the light out. It's a kind of hot, pungent dread. A metally taste in my mouth.

Portia   Fear. Fear is what you're talking about.

Jack   I lost my mother seventy years ago and I can still remember the scent of the soap she used.

Portia   What was she like, your mother?

Jack   To tell you the truth, I can't remember. Just bits. The smell of her. The feel of her. She used to let me nuzzle her ear. But at night, now . . .

Portia   What?

Jack   I remember things. Piercing things, and I don't know why they're coming back to me now. Time's turning inside out.

Portia   Sometimes I wake up and I forget Joe's been dead for five years.

Jack   We were dirt poor, my mother and me after my father died. That hard, bitter, shameful poverty. I smelt, I know I did. And I saved up all these little bits of money until I had a shilling, and said to my mother, 'Here, I saved this up, you can have it, it's for you' and she said, 'No, you keep it, son, it's your money, you keep it.' So I spent it on toffees, and a frog that croaked when you wound it up. And she crept into my bedroom late that night, and said, 'Jack, are you asleep? D'you still have that money? Could I borrow it? I'll pay you back.' I could tell she'd been crying, but I couldn't give her the money because I'd spent it. I knew that if she'd had to ask, she must have needed it very badly, and my mouth was sticky with toffee and shame. And she was ashamed too, that she'd had to ask me. And every night now, it catches my breath. It pierces my heart that I bought toffees and a frog, and my mother sitting wretched downstairs. Two months later she was dead.

Portia   Your mother probably forgot about it long before you did.

Jack   She didn't have much choice, she was dead.

Portia   You were a child. It wasn't your fault.

Silence.

Jack   What time is it?

Portia *looks at her watch.*

Portia   Half past eleven. Why?

He pours himself a large whisky from a bottle next to him.

Jack   Will you have one?

Portia   Too early for me.

Jack   I'm past caring.

He takes a swig.

Jack   What I liked about maps, was they pinned things down. Put things in order. You don't feel you're bobbing around on a sea of nothing. There's a shape to the world. Something to hold onto. That's what I liked about them.

Portia   You're talking in the past tense.

Jack   I'm not sure anymore. I've lost my bearings a bit.

Pause.

I don't know why I told you that about my mother. Sorry.

Portia   What's to be sorry about?

Jack   I don't really hate abroad you know. The children think I do, but it's not that I hate it, it's just that I don't want to go there anymore.

Portia   Where?

Jack   Anywhere. I came back and I made a home for myself and my family. I stayed put and I made a life. I collected my maps. I dug up my family tree. I kept a handle on it all. I made this person that I am now.

Portia   You said you came back. From where?

Jack   I had a bit of a run in. In Aden.

Portia   When?

Jack   It was years ago. Before the children were born. I was there a year. Bookkeeping for an engineering firm. I was young. Twenty-two or something. I knew nothing about anything. I'm not sure I even knew which country I was in. You just went there and did your job. And they waited on you. The natives. Brought you drinks and did your washing, cooked your food. I'd known nothing like it. I felt like a lord.

Portia   So. You had a run in. What does that mean?

Jack   Have you ever been to Aden?

Portia   It's in Yemen, isn't it?

Pause.

Your map with the fountains and camels. That's Yemen, isn't it?

Jack   Yes. It's very hot. I came out in a prickly rash. The skin would just peel off you.

Pause.

I did something terrible.

Portia   You did?

Jack   Yes.

Pause.

The water wasn't good. You couldn't drink it. So we'd drink beer, whisky, that sort of thing. I suppose . . . anyway I must have had too much. I don't remember feeling drunk. But we were probably drunk most of the time. Driving around on a motor scooter. I had a car as well. A Morris Oxford. I'm not sure I even passed a test. They gave me a car so I drove it. It was like the Wild West.

Pause.

When I went into him it was like a dream. He was nowhere
and suddenly there he was, cartwheeling over the bonnet.
That's what it looked like. A cartwheel. I can still see it:
those loose black arms and legs wheeling in slow motion. It
was almost beautiful. Then thud. A sort of crunching sound.
I stuffed my foot on the brake and got out. Beer and bile
rushed up from my stomach. Pints of it, gushed out onto the
dust. And above it all this sweet perfumed smell. I looked
over and he was lying all wrong. Everything the wrong way
round. He'd been carrying a bottle of Bombay Sapphire gin.
Must have been an errand for one of us. He still had the
broken neck of the bottle in his hand. There were shards of
turquoise blue glass twinkling all around him and that
strange cocktail bar smell made the whole thing almost
festive. But there was a thick blood smell underneath, like a
dry martini in a slaughterhouse. He looked about ten years
old.

Portia   What happened to him? Did he die?

Jack   He was dead right there in the road. I knew. His legs
were the wrong way round.

Portia   Who was he?

Jack   They took him away. Cleaned me up. The next day
they sent me home on sick leave. They never had a name
for him. He was just some black boy. It didn't really matter,
you see? It was as if I'd run over a dog. After a while I
thought maybe I'd dreamt it. Had it actually happened. No-
one mentioned it. And I never told a soul. Not even my
wife.

Portia   Couldn't you have done something? You could
have found out who he was, you could have, I don't know,
you could have –

Jack   I could have done all sorts of things. I didn't do
anything. Life went on. Minute by minute, day after day,
moon after moon, the way it does. My life went on, and his
stopped in its tracks. Except something about it went on, in

parallel with mine. A virtual life. A virtual death. He'd be in his fifties now.

Portia   I'm shocked you're telling me this, Jack. I'm shocked it happened but I'm more shocked that you choose to pass the baton to me. Why? To what do I owe the honour?

Jack   I'm not passing the baton. I've been carrying it for fifty years and I'm still carrying it.

Portia   Were you hoping I'd offer you forgiveness?

Jack   If I wanted absolution I'd have told Father Ryan.

Portia   So what is it you want?

Jack   I don't know. I don't know why I'm telling you and not someone else. You don't always know why you do things.

Pause.

Portia   In this country you'd have gone to prison. Even then.

Jack   I should have done. If I could go back, I'd say put me away, punish me, make me pay for this in a way that's finite and concrete and graspable. Make me think of his blotted out life every minute of every day for five years, ten years, whatever it's to be, and then let it be over.

Portia   So why did you never do that Jack? Why did you never put up your hand and say I'll take my punishment?

Jack   It would have been like shouting down a well, all I'd get back was my own echo. Nobody cared. I accidentally killed a black houseboy who didn't seem to belong to anyone. So what? The 'So what?' is what I'm carrying. So fucking what.

Pause.

Portia   Is it realer now than it was then?

Jack   It was a shadow mostly. But now time's imploding and all sorts of moments rush at me. I can taste these things in my mouth, I can smell things I thought I'd forgotten. It doesn't seem like memory. It seems real. It feels as if time's turning inside out.

Portia   So now you've told me. What d'you want me to do?

Jack   I've no idea.

Portia   D'you feel better?

Pause.

Jack   No.

Pause.

Jack   I'm sorry, that's not your fault.

Portia   I'm not stupid enough to think it was.

Jack   So what d'you make of me now?

Portia   You were twenty-two years old. You were ignorant, and you were drunk. I wish it hadn't happened. For his sake, and for yours. What else can I say?

Jack   I think of all the ways it could have been avoided. Not being drunk, obviously. Not having sat next to Percy Collingwood at school who ten years later, got me the job that took me to Aden in the first place. If the shopkeeper had been a bit slower handing him the change for the gin. Or a bit faster. He wouldn't have been crossing the road at that moment. If –

Portia   – you hadn't been born. If your parents hadn't met. If Britain hadn't had an empire. If, if, if.

Jack   But it's the other possibilities that unhinge me. All those alternative outcomes. And did all the things that didn't happen somehow contribute to the thing that did? Is the road you didn't take as vital as the road you did take? Is the one you chose contingent upon the one you rejected? D'you see?

Portia   I think you should stop doing this, Jack, or your head will explode.

Jack   It's hard to stop once you start. Try it.

Portia   I won't, thanks. If everything you do or don't do is contingent upon everything else you do or don't do, you'll never manage to do anything. You'll be in a state of paralysis.

Jack   It was Father Ryan that started me off on this track.

Portia   Well he should be shot.

Jack   With his quantum physics. Which frankly I don't think he understands or he would never have lent me the book in the first place. All I can say is it hasn't helped.

Portia   He should have been giving you the Bible to read.

Jack   He reads all kinds of stuff. Hinduism, Islam, Buddhism, they're all at it these days.

Portia   Well you know what they say: an interest in comparative religion is the first sign of insanity.

Pause.

You're smiling now. Which means you can put these griefs aside if you want to.

Jack   Not aside. They're still there but you can't see them. The thing's always with me. For years I was afraid it had altered the shape of my cells, got into my DNA, like a stain. When Michael was born I had this terror he may have inherited it. Like a black spot.

Portia *picks up a saucer.*

Portia   Here, spit into this.

Jack   What?

Portia   Say the terrible thing that you did and spit into this.

Jack *takes the saucer, warily.*

Portia   Go on.

Pause.

Jack   I killed someone.

He spits into the saucer. **Portia** *takes it back from him.*

Portia   He killed someone.

She spits into the saucer. Then she takes it to the garden tap and flushes it away.

Portia   There. Done.

Jack   Will that change anything?

Portia   No. But you didn't want it and I didn't want it, so I flushed it away. One small step. It washes the stain off the afternoon, that's all.

Lights down. Music.

Lights up, garden, afternoon.

Jack *is asleep in his electric wheelchair. His head is lolling and he's wearing a sun hat.* **Michael** *and* **Sholto** *are polishing glasses from a huge box.*

Michael   Sorry about last night.

Sholto   I thought it was quite funny.

Michael   I had such a headache when I woke up I thought I'd gone blind.

Sholto   What's he got against actors?

Michael   I don't think it *is* because I'm an actor actually. I think that's just the excuse. It's something else.

Sholto   Like what?

Michael   I haven't a clue. Maybe I remind him of someone, I don't know. Anna's the one he loves unconditionally, and I'm the one who's a bit of an irritant. It's always been like that.

Jack's head lolls further and the hat drops off his head onto the ground.

Michael   His head'll get burnt –

Sholto   I'll do it –

He goes over and puts the hat back on Jack's head. Jack stirs. He stares at Sholto through sleep clouded eyes.

Jack   What do you want?

Sholto   Your hat fell off.

Jack tries to shake himself awake.

Jack   Who are you?

Michael   It's Sholto, Dad, who d'you think it is?

Jack leans away from Sholto.

Jack   I haven't got any money.

Sholto   It's OK, I don't want any money. Go back to sleep.

Pause. Jack looks at him, confused.

Jack   Am I still asleep?

Sholto   I think you're having a bad dream Jack.

Jack   Anna!

Michael   Go back to sleep, Dad.

Jack (*still looking at Sholto*)   Who are you?

Sholto   It's me, Sholto, it's OK.

He moves to Jack, hand outstretched. Jack shies away.

Jack   I'm still asleep. I know this is a dream, and I know who you are.

Sholto   I'm Sholto.

Jack   You speak very good English.

Michael   He's about to become your son-in-law.

Jack   I don't like the look of you.

Sholto   I'm sorry about that.

Jack   Have you ever been in Aden?

Sholto   No.

Michael *goes over and looks at* **Jack**.

Michael   D'you think he's had a stroke?

Jack   Are you sure you've never been in Aden?

Sholto   I don't even know where it is.

Jack   In that case I'm awake.

He shakes himself.

Jack   I'm sorry. I thought I was dreaming. Was I dreaming?

Sholto   Sort of.

Michael   Shall I get you a drink?

Jack   Are you still drunk?

Michael   No, I'm hungover. What can I get you?

Jack   Just water.

He goes to get **Jack** *water from the table.*

Jack   I'm sorry, Sholto. I thought you were someone else.

Sholto   Who?

Jack   Someone from way back. Sorry. I feel a bit shaky.

Michael *brings him the water and he gulps it.*

Jack   Thank you.

Michael   You all right now?

Jack   Better. Thank you.

He hands the glass back.

Jack   It's all different now. Nothing's the way it was. I never dreamt I'd have a daughter who was a lawyer and a son-in-law who was a . . . also a lawyer. I thought Michael was going to be the one in the law.

Sholto   You should leave him alone.

Jack   I know.

Michael   Sorry, could you say that again? In fact, could you put it in writing?

Sholto   So why d'you do it to him then?

Michael   It's OK, Sholto, forget it, leave him –

Jack   I don't know. I can't help it.

Michael   Well at least you're admitting it, that's a start.

Jack   You irritate me sometimes.

Michael   You irritate me sometimes. That's what people do in families. It's par for the course.

Jack   I mean to say nice things to him and nasty things come out. I can't help it. We brush each other up the wrong way.

Sholto   Couldn't you just drop it for a while, Jack?

Jack   Wait till you have children. You think it's going to be unalloyed love and it's not. There's scratchy stuff. You see things in them you don't like.

Sholto   Bits of yourself.

Jack   Possibly.

Michael   Christ, are you suggesting I'm like you?

Jack   I don't know, I'm just saying it's different with sons because . . . because sons are more . . . you see yourself more, that's all. I need one of my tablets. Or a whisky. I need a painkiller.

Michael *pours him a whisky from the bottle next to his chair.*

Michael   There you are.

Jack *takes it and rests his hand on* **Michael***'s, for a few seconds. It's a tiny, yet huge gesture.* **Jack** *raises his glass to* **Sholto***.*

Jack   Anna told me. Congratulations.

Michael   Anna told you what?

Jack   I'm about to have my first grandchild.

Michael   Oh. No-one told me.

Jack   What colour d'you think it will be? I mean, sort of coffee, or more of a honey colour?

Sholto   Is it important?

Jack   Probably not.

Sholto   All we know is it probably won't be white Jack.

Jack   You're right. It's not important. I was just trying to imagine it, that's all, because I probably won't get to, you know . . .

Pause.

Sholto   I know.

Michael   We know, Dad. It's all right.

Jack *looks at him.*

Jack   I don't want Anna to be upset. Not just before her wedding. So let's keep it from her, all right?

Sholto   We won't say a word, Jack.

Pause.

Jack   If you've got the time, Michael, d'you think you could teach me to play poker?

Michael   Sure. It's not actually that difficult.

Jack   Just brush me up on the rules and we'll have a hand later.

Michael   And then you'll probably beat me.

Jack   I bloody hope so. What's the point otherwise? It's too hot out here. Can someone help me inside?

Sholto   Sure, Jack –

*He takes **Jack**'s arm, and guides him in, as **Anna** comes out.*

Jack   I'm going for a lie down.

*They go. **Michael** looks at **Anna**.*

Michael   Why didn't you tell me you were pregnant?

Anna   Because I only told Sholto the day before yesterday.

Michael   Oh.

He shuffles.

He told Dad though. Why didn't he tell me?

Anna   Jesus, Michael I don't know. Does it matter?

Michael   I was the last person to know you were getting married as well.

Anna   I only found out you were getting divorced because your wife told me –

Michael   That's because I was pretending it wasn't happening.

Anna   Anyway, I'm sorry we didn't tell you straight away but these things are complicated at my age. And now you know, so stop complaining and would you like to be its godfather?

Michael   Are you serious?

Anna   Black godmother – Sholto's sister, white godfather – you. It appealed to our sense of symmetry.

Michael   Do I have to say things like, 'I renounce the Devil'?

Anna   No. Purely secular.

Michael   Yeah. All right then. I'd love to.

Pause.

D'you think I'll be any good at it?

Anna   No, you'll be crap, we only asked you because we feel sorry for you, what do you think?

Michael   God . . . it's bit daunting . . . am I supposed to be cultural ambassador for the whiteys?

Anna   Yeah. We'd like you to teach her about Morris dancing.

Michael   Seriously. What am I going to bring to the poor fucker? Last Night of the Proms? Harris tweed?

Anna   Fortrum and Mason

Michael   Turnbnell and Asser.

Anna   Pinky and Perky.

Michael   Charles and Camilla.

Anna   A culture, finely crafted out of purest porcelain –

Michael   – stamped, franked, and authenticated by experts –

Anna   – for you to cherish in absurdam – ten ninety-nine a month for the rest of you life.

Michael   Deluxe version available in old gold. With a coronet.

Anna   Economy version available in man-made fibre. Lightly dusted with a Class A narcotic of your choice.

Michael   Did you just call it 'her?'

Anna   I have an irrational feeling it's a girl. I've even thought of a name for her.

Michael   What?

Anna   Dido. What d'you think?

Lights down.

Lights up on garden. Evening, present day. From the house come sounds of music and partying. There are lights twinkling in the trees and white balloons strewn around the ground. Empty champagne bottles and glasses litter the place. **Jack** *is sitting in a garden chair, wearing a smart suits and tie, with a carnation in his buttonhole. He is drinking whiskey, and there's a bottle in front of him on the table.* **Father Ryan** *comes out, clutching a glass.*

Father Ryan   Ah, Jack, there you are.

Jack   Too noisy in there.

Father Ryan   How are you?

Jack   Never felt better.

Father Ryan *draws a garden chair up.*

Father Ryan   It seemed to go off well.

Jack   Let's hope it lasts.

Father Ryan   What?

Jack   The marriage. Michael didn't manage it.

Father Ryan   Ah well.

He downs his drink.

Jack   Help yourself to another.

Father Ryan   Thanks Jack, I will.

He pours himself another drink.

Jack   So, what do you want? D'you want to assuage me with the consolations of religion and the sure and certain knowledge of the Resurrection?

Father Ryan   Not at all.

Jack   Go on.

Father Ryan   No.

Jack   I thought that was your bloody job. Go on. Tell me I'll be up there with the angels and a bottle of Scotch by the end of the month.

Father Ryan *sips his drink.*

Father Ryan   I wish I could.

Jack   What?

Father Ryan   I've had a few drinks, Jack.

Jack   So've we all.

Father Ryan   D'you think you'll see Rose again, Jack? D'you think she's waiting for you on the other side?

Pause.

Jack   D'you want the truth? No.

Pause.

Father Ryan   Neither do I.

Jack   What?

Father Ryan *picks up the bottle.*

Father Ryan   D'you mind if I have another one of these?

Jack   Give me one while you're at it –

He winces in pain as he reaches out.

Father Ryan   Are you all right there, Jack?

Jack   Just a twinge. The tablets are pretty good.

He takes his whisky. **Father Ryan** *downs his and stares into the glass.*

Father Ryan   I'm leaving the Church, Jack.

Jack   You're what?

Father Ryan   I've lost my faith.

Jack   You can't have lost it.

Father Ryan   I have.

Jack   I've been relying on you.

Father Ryan   I'm sorry.

Jack   You were the one certain thing. I was spoiling for a fight with you. I had it all planned. You were going to persuade me at the last minute, and I was going to cave in.

Father Ryan   What was I going to persuade you of?

Jack   That there was something more. That death wasn't the end.

Father Ryan   At least you can say the 'd' word now Jack. That's a step in the right direction.

Jack   You've let me down.

Father Ryan   I'm sorry.

Silence.

Jack   Is this a sudden thing, this loss of faith?

Father Ryan   It's been a slow drip. And then one morning I woke up and whatever it was that kept me in the priesthood had gone. Like an amputation. I can still feel the phantom limb but I know it's not real.

Pause.

Jack   I wish you'd never lent me those bloody books.

Father Ryan   Doesn't it comfort you, Jack? That it's all just as mysterious and unknowable as we were always taught. Just in a different way that's all. We're all stardust.

Jack   Did you see the map they gave me? The map of my life?

Father Ryan   I did. I don't know why but it made me cry.

Jack   I thought when I saw it, is that all there is? Is that all I was? Because I know in my heart there are other things that don't fit in there. There were other things in my life that no-one knows about. But the map is the life I mostly lived. There's another one in my head, but what I lived was that. And it choked me because that was my real life and I realised how small it was. And I can't change it now. There are no more choices to make.

Pause.

Jack   D'you think there's another version of my life out there where different choices were made?

Father Ryan   Would you like that, Jack?

Jack   More than anything.

Father Ryan   Then I hope so.

Anna *and* **Sholto** *come out, followed by* **Michael**, **Anna** *and* **Portia**, *all in their wedding finery, except that* **Anna** *has taken off her shoes. They are all a little tipsy and in high spirits.*

Anna   Oh my poor feet, I'm so glad I got rid of those shoes –

She throws herself down in a chair.

Anna   What are you doing out here, Dad? You're missing the party.

Jack   I'm talking to Father Ryan.

She goes to **Jack** *and puts her arms around him.*

Anna   Are you exhausted? Has it all been too much?

Jack *winces and smiles.*

Jack   I'm fine, get off –

Father Ryan *gets up.*

Father Ryan   I'll better be off then, Jack –

Jack   No, don't, stay.

Michael   You'll miss the dancing.

Father Ryan   I've danced with the bridesmaids twice, that'll do me.

Anna   No, Sholto's dance – He arranged it specially for the wedding, with a band and everything, they're getting ready now –

Sholto   I'd better go and keep an eye on them actually, I don't want them getting too drunk.

He goes.

Father Ryan   I'll hang on then in that case. It's been a great day, hasn't it?

Jack *is patting his pockets, trying to find something.*

Jack   Portia? There's a packet on my bedside table with my tablets in it. Bring it down will you?

Anna   I'll get it, Dad.

Jack   No, no, Portia'll get it, won't you?

Portia   Of course I will, Jack.

She goes.

Anna   You've had all your tablets haven't you?

Jack   I missed a couple. The pain's a bit, you know . . .

Anna   D'you want to come inside? Maybe you should be inside –

Jack   I'm fine here. I'm fine where I am. You go in and enjoy yourselves. Where's this dance going to be?

Michael   Out here.

Jack   I'll be here. With Father Ryan. You go on in.

Anna   OK . . .

They go in reluctantly. **Jack** *looks at* **Father Ryan**.

Jack   Got a cigarette?

Father Ryan   I've got one somewhere.

He digs out a packet and lights one for **Jack**.

Jack   Fine time to tell me you've lost your faith, that's all I can say.

Father Ryan   Sorry, Jack. I shouldn't have done that. It's the drink. It slipped out.

Jack   You could have let it slip out with someone else. Someone who wasn't about to find out for themselves there's nothing out there.

Father Ryan   Sorry, Jack.

He takes a long drag.

Jack   A neutron starts out as a particle, travels as a wave, and arrives as a particle.

Father Ryan   That's about the size of it.

Pause.

Jack   How you going to manage without it?

Father Ryan   What?

Jack   Faith.

Father Ryan   I'm hoping there might be other consolations.

Jack   Like sex, you mean?

Father Ryan   I hadn't thought of that at all. I'm just looking forward to being irresponsible for once, although I haven't actually worked out how that might manifest itself. It'll be great not having to be wise all the time. Or compassionate. It'll be great saying to some whinging old sod, 'Ah shut up, will you, you miserable fecker.' I might take up a hobby. Fishing or something.

Jack   Not much of a swap. The joy of fishing in exchange for the glory of life everlasting.

Father Ryan   No. It's not much of a swap. But what can I do?

Jack   Fuck all.

He knocks back his drink.

Jack   Now you've lost your faith I can swear to my heart's content.

Father Ryan   Actually Jack, you always did.

Portia *comes out.*

Portia   Is this what you wanted Jack?

She hands him a brown paper bag. **Jack** *takes it and looks inside.*

Jack   That's it. Thank you.

He gives a sharp intake of breath.

Portia   Is the pain bad?

Jack   A bit.

Father Ryan   Why didn't you say, Jack? I've been banging on about myself, and here's you in pain.

Jack   Seems a funny time to be dying doesn't it. A wedding. They're just starting out and I'm just leaving.

He loosens his tie.

Portia   You're not going just yet Jack.

Jack   No, not quite.

He pats his packet of tablets.

Jack   Just a comfort blanket, you know?

Portia *sits down and holds his hand.*

Portia   Sholto'll be starting the dancing soon.

Jack   Rose and I used to dance. Old fashioned stuff. The fox trot. She taught me that. And waltzing. Can you dance Portia?

Portia   A bit.

Jack *gets to his feet.*

Jack   Here –

He holds out his arms to her.

Father Ryan   You sit down, Jack, you're in no state for dancing.

He holds out his arms. He's shaky.

Jack   The last waltz. Make my day.

Portia   All right then, Jack.

*The map of **Jack**'s life appears on the screens, as does the fantasy map of Yemen. Both get clearer and more intense as the scene progresses. **Portia** takes his hand and they waltz slowly, to the sounds of music from inside the house.*

Jack   I started out as a particle, travelled as a wave, and I'll arrive as a particle . . .

*Slowly the music fades and is replaced by the sounds of **Sholto**'s band warming up. **Jack** and **Portia** waltz slowly and painfully back to the seat as **Anna** and **Michael** run out and the band strikes up its rhythmic beat. **Sholto** and his dancers tumble onto the stage and the dance begins. Everyone watches rapturously. At the side **Jack** watches, smiling. **Portia** sits next to him, hand on his shoulder. **Jack** and **Portia** watch, as **Jack** clutches the bag of tablets. The dancers whirl and fly. The music roars and pounds. The map of*

Printed in the USA
CPSIA information can be obtained
at www.ICGtesting.com
LVHW041100171024
794057LV00001B/182